# Living Wicca Today
## Pagan Holidays & Earth Magic

Print Edition of eBooks 1 & 2 in the Series

Kardia Zoe

# DEDICATION

This book is dedicated to you, my reader. You are my true source of inspiration and motivation to continue writing. I love sharing my insight into Wicca with you and it is my hope that you'll experience the same magic on this path that I do. If you find the information helpful, please help me in return by leaving a review for this book on Amazon. Thank you so much! Peace and health be with you, Kardia

# ACKNOWLEDGMENTS

The information in this book draws from our popular Living Wicca Today publications, articles Kardia has written over the past ten years for the Inner Circle newsletter and material written for our website: http://wicca.com .

# TABLE OF CONTENTS

# PART 1 : WICCAN & PAGAN HOLIDAYS

An Easy Beginner's Guide to Celebrating the Sabbats and Esbats

*The heavens smile, the earth celebrates, the morning stars sing together, and all the Children of Light shout for Joy.*

From The Unknown Books of the Essenes

# Getting Started

Are you new to Wicca and need an easy, accurate guide to celebrating the Sabbats and Esbats? Perhaps you turned to Wicca years ago but your life just seems too busy now for special celebrations and rituals. This guide offers beginners and solitary practitioners simple ways to live a magical life by connecting (or reconnecting) with the Divine in Nature.

The benefits of living in harmony with the Earth and celebrating her cycles are incredible. When we take care of her and honor her ancient wisdom, she shares her secrets with us and leads us to a life of blessings that include a healthier body, a peaceful mind and a joyful spirit.

As you gain an understanding of the ancient celebrations, you'll discover new ways to keep the old traditions alive. While Wiccan and Pagan traditions vary greatly, most tend to focus on the Goddess and God and on our home, the Earth. As you begin to attune yourself with the seasons of the Earth, you'll experience her magic in meaningful and satisfying ways. Are you ready to get started?

# The "Practice" of Wicca

If someone tells you they love the teachings of Wicca, but they don't practice it, they usually mean they don't celebrate the Sabbats or do Esbat rituals. There are 21 Wiccan occasions, (8 solar Sabbats and 13 lunar Esbats), and with so many different traditions and rituals for each occasion, the beginner or solitary practitioner can easily get confused.

This guide offers you a brief description of each Sabbat and Esbat, along with simple activities and foods for each event. You'll find ample ideas on how to celebrate your sacred days and nights throughout the year. Of course you are not obligated to celebrate them all, but each one is an opportunity to strengthen your connection with Mother Earth and her Divine power.

I have friends who are adamant about keeping their Sabbat rituals traditional. Some believe that if you don't follow all the traditions, you should not call yourself a Wiccan or Witch. Others have a different view.

One reader told me *"Sitting alone in my garden, staring at the full moon and feeling how beautiful and how powerful is, this is one of my rituals. My everyday ritual is to try my best to be a good person, take care of Nature and feel every blessing Nature returns to me! I don't do rituals for the Sabbats or anything else, but I still feel that I'm a witch and I feel that I'm connected."* I could not agree more!

That's all the Divine wants from us...a heart that is aware of the Earth's gifts and thankful for those simple blessings! If we put too much focus on duplicating the actions of others in our celebrations, it's easy to lose sight of the true reason we are celebrating.

To be clear, if the ancient tools and traditions hold a deep meaning for you personally, then of course you should keep them in your celebrations. But for many, concern about recreating the exact traditions of the past can diminish the joy and beauty of the holiday and even cause them to avoid celebrating altogether. Don't let this happen! If this is how you feel, simply focus on celebrating your *PERSONAL* connection with the Divine.

# Preparing for Your Celebrations

Many of us like to set up an altar and scent the air with incense or oils when we talk to our Goddess or God, in the same way we might set our table and put on a pot of coffee when we invite a friend over to visit. These things set the mood and help make the time we spend together extra special. But just as a true friend will gladly come over to talk without being served refreshments, so will the Divine be there for you, without all the ritual settings.

Celebrating the Sabbats can get complicated with special foods, activities and decorations involved. For some, eliminating these things is like trying to hold a Yule celebration without a tree or gifts. Keeping old traditions are what these events are really all about … right? Well … traditions certainly DO make the events special, but our ancestors observed the Sabbats to help them stay in tune with the changing seasons and to celebrate the blessings those changes brought. This is where our focus should be!

A great way to honor the Divine is to share the season's harvest. That could be fresh flowers and herbs or berries and produce, whatever gifts our Earthly Mother is providing us. Our activities should also center on the changing seasons. Walking in the woods to collect May flowers or gathering wood for a fire on a cold October night are activities that can connect us with Nature. These things help us celebrate the season and give us a chance to thank the Divine for the many blessings each season bring us.

We should connect with our God or Goddess in a way that feels right to us. Many find that connection through Nature, but others find it through a craft or form of art. Writing, painting, photography, woodworking or singing and dancing are a just a few activities that allow us to express our spiritual connection with the Divine and share it with others.

Music and dance have long been used in magical and religious ceremonies. Many believe these activities can raise power, alter consciousness and help them unite with the God and Goddess.

In his book Wicca: A Guide for the Solitary Practitioner, Scott Cunningham writes, *"Music is simply a re-creation of the sounds of nature. Wind through the trees, the roar of the ocean hurling itself against jagged cliffs, pattering rain, crackling of a lightning produced fire, the cry of birds and roars of animals are some of the 'instruments' that constitute the music of nature."*

There are an unlimited number of ways to incorporate sound into your activities. As with everything else, the best music, tools or activities for your rituals will depend on what feels right to you. If something helps you connect with the spirit of the Divine, then don't worry if it's not what others are doing or if it's not in the book you just read.

In Wicca, how you choose to practice your religion is between you and your God or Goddess. As long as you abide by the Wiccan Rede, your celebrations and rituals will honor the Divine.

These Eight words the Rede fulfill:

**"An Ye Harm None, Do What Ye Will"**

The full version of the Wiccan Rede can be found here:

http://wicca.com/celtic/wicca/rede.htm

## The Reason for the Season

The Sabbat is sometimes referred to as a Witches' Sabbath. The word means "to rest." It is a time to set work aside and simply celebrate the transformation of the season.

Our ancestors saw the Sabbats as happy times. Entire communities would set their work aside and gather to honor their deities and celebrate the season. Originally the Sabbats were dates that marked our planting and harvesting times but over the years, as we became less reliant on hunting and farming for survival, the Sabbats slowly turned into religious and celebratory holidays.

If you prefer to be alone, you should be alone, and if you want to be part of a group celebration but know no other pagans, then simply throw a party to honor the day. Don't worry about special Sabbat rituals. The most important thing is to acknowledge the season and its meaning. Focus on celebrating the turning of the Wheel of the Year and honor the cycle of life.

Don't worry about doing the wrong thing. Relax. Take a break from your usual routine. Light a candle and celebrate with a joyful heart as you give thanks for the seasonal blessings of the Goddess and God.

Tip: If you want to do magical work at this time, it's a good practice to perform your spells just prior to the Sabbat so you can simply relax and enjoy a day of fun.

# As the Wheel Turns

The Wheel of the Year is a Neo-pagan term used to describe the annual cycle of the Earth's seasons, and it tells the story of the life of the God and Goddess. In most traditions, the Goddess or Mother Earth is the God's Consort or companion.

In this cycle, the God (Sun) is reborn each Yule, (Winter Solstice) after the longest night of the year. As the days become longer, he grows in power and warms the cold Earth. She awakens from her slumber to renew and flourish. Then on Litha (Summer Solstice), the God dies again and the days begin to grow shorter. As the Sun's power fades, the Earth falls asleep and waits for his rebirth on the next Winter Solstice.

Our ancestors adjusted their lives to these seasonal changes. They followed both the solar and lunar cycles of the year. These ever-changing cycles became known as the Wheel of the Year.

There are eight Sabbats. Four of them, sometimes referred to as the Greater Sabbats, are based on old Celtic festivals. The other four, or lesser Sabbats, are based on the first days of the four seasons. These are also known as solstices and equinoxes.

A solstice is the time of year when the sun reaches its highest or lowest point in the sky, marking the longest and shortest days of the year. In the northern hemisphere, the summer solstice is celebrated around June 21, when the sun reaches its northernmost point on the celestial sphere. The winter solstice happens around December 22. Due to seasonal differences, these celebrations are reversed in the southern hemisphere.

The word equinox is derived from the Latin equus (equal) and nox (night). An equinox happens twice a year when night and day are about the same length. The Sun is crossing the Equator (an imaginary line around the middle of the Earth) and it is an equal distance from the North Pole and the South Pole. Since summer and winter seasons are opposite on either side of the equator in the northern hemisphere the equinox in September is known as the "autumnal (fall) equinox". However, in the southern hemisphere, September is the time of the "spring (vernal) equinox".

Although astronomically the solstices and equinoxes mark the beginning of the seasons, to our ancestors, they actually represented the midpoint of each season. This is why October 31 to November 1 (Samhain) was traditionally celebrated as the end of fall and the beginning of winter, while the Winter solstice was considered the midpoint of winter. Spring began on February 2 (Imbolc), summer on May 1 (Beltane), and autumn on August 1 (Lughnasadh or Lammas).

It's important to note that these dates are not the same around the world. The Sabbat dates in this book are for the Northern Hemisphere. In the Southern Hemisphere these festivals are commonly shifted by six months to match the local seasons. You will want to adjust your celebrations accordingly.

Keeping in tune with nature's cycles may sound a bit complicated, but it's not. The bottom line is to simply celebrate the change in seasons and enjoy whatever activity is appropriate for the current time of year in YOUR part of the world. And don't make your rituals too complicated. They should be fun and a true expression of thankfulness for what is to come.

Your Sabbat celebrations and Esbat rituals should always express your love and appreciation for nature. Be sure to give thanks for all the little blessings in your life, like the soft grass beneath your feet, the colorful flowers in your garden or an old tree that provides you with shelter from the weather. Being grateful for the blessings we have already received can cast a transforming blanket of joy and peace over our mundane life experiences.

In Wicca, the "THREE-FOLD LAW OF RETURN" or "LAW OF THREE" teaches that whatever we do, for good or ill, will be returned to us threefold. Thus, the very act of sending thoughts and feelings of gratitude out will guarantee that you'll have even more to be grateful about in the future. The more things you find to be thankful for, the faster new Divine blessings will start flowing into your life. This is a well-known Universal Law also referred to as the Law of Attraction!

If your rituals seem empty because you simply memorize words and perform activities that have no meaning to you, there is not much benefit in doing them. One reader shared with me that she did not need a special altar or a certain color candle for special occasions. All she needed was to be outside and concentrate on a flower, a star, the moon, the warmth of the sun, the cool earth, or listen to some rippling water to feel connected to all that grows and lives.

This person is simply doing what feels right to her. It's up to you whether you celebrate the seasons or not, but if you do, choose activities, rituals and/or foods that make each occasion enjoyable for YOU.

Tip: If you miss the exact day or time that a Sabbat is normally celebrated, it's not the end of the world. What's MOST important is to celebrate when you can. Strive continually to balance your life with the rhythms of the natural world. Every time you stop to observe nature's cycles and take part in an activity that honors the change in the season, the ordinary becomes extraordinary and your life becomes more magical.

# Sabbats and Children

I was talking to my daughter (now 30) about teaching Wicca to children. Her dad, Herne, believed that being a Wiccan or Witch meant you were a healer, a teacher, a seeker, a giver, and a protector of all things. He felt that walking the old paths meant "...being in the presence of Mother Earth's nature and being humbled in reverence." For us, teaching Wicca to children was not about teaching spells and rituals. It was about helping them connect with our mother Earth. Our focus should always be on teaching nature's cycles and rhythms, and helping others, both young and old, learn to respect, honor and work with all living things.

No one knows more about having fun and celebrating the moment than a child. My favorite book on connecting with nature was written by a child. After reading a few paragraphs from this book it was clear that children could teach adults a lot about following a nature-based magical path.

Excerpts from this child's writing are listed below. She grew up in the woods of western Oregon and in her diary (written when she was 6 - 7 years old) she recorded a world alive with creatures, fairies, talking trees, and singing creeks. Here are a few of her words:

The wind ... calls to me to come go exploring. It sings of the things that are to be found under leaves. It whispers the dreams of the tall fir trees. It does pipe the gentle song the forest sings on gray days. I hear all the voices calling me. I listen...

The wind does have many things to tell. He does toss back one's curls so he can whisper things in one's ears. Today he did push back my curls three times, that I might better hear what he did have to say.

"I wave greetings to the plant-bush folks that do dance all about. Today a grand pine tree did wave its arms to me. And the bush branches patted my cheek in a friendly way."

"Raindrops were beginning to come down from the sky. Their coming was in a gentle way. I had longs to be out with them. I so do like to feel the raindrops patter on my head and I like to run runs and hold out my hands to meet them."

For this little girl, something magical was always happening right outside her front door. Most children experience this enthusiasm for the natural world. We should think of ourselves as Leaders of Learning when we explore our Mother Earth's gifts with them. If we are lucky, as we share our knowledge of the old traditions, moon lore and nature's changing seasons with our children, they might teach US something about the true spirit and magic at the heart of these wonderful celebrations!

***Blessed is the Child of Light
who is wise in mind,
for he shall create heaven.***

*The mind of the wise is a well-ploughed field,
which giveth forth abundance and plenty.*

*For if thou show a handful of seed to a wise man,
he will see in his mind's eye
a field of golden wheat.*

*And if thou show a handful of seed to a fool,
he will see only that which is before him,
and call them worthless pebbles.*

*And as the field of the wise man giveth forth
grain in abundance,
and the field of the fool is a harvest
only of stones,*
***So it is with our thoughts!***

Excerpt from *The Unknown Books of the Essenes*

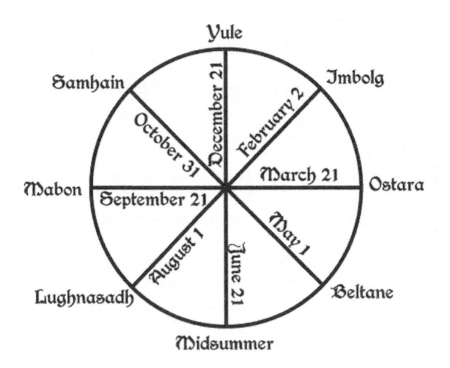

# THE SABBAT TRADITIONS

Your magical journey will continue as you reconnect with the Divine through nature. In the next section of this book you'll find a chapter for each Sabbat with lore, suggested activities and recipes to help you celebrate the day!

As you explore the traditions in this book, keep in mind that all customs, like the people who observe them, tend to evolve over time. The information shared here should be used as a guide, not as Divine law. Plan your personal celebrations accordingly!

NOTE: Since the traditional Wiccan year begins on Oct 31st, the Sabbat listings in this book will begin with Samhain.

## Samhain Traditions

Samhain, (pronounced SOW-in, SAH-vin, or SAM-hayne) means "End of Summer" and marks the third and final Harvest. Other common names for this Greater Sabbat are Third Harvest, Day of the Dead and All Hallow's Eve. Today, Samhain is commonly considered the Witch's New Year.

**Note:** You may encounter some witches and traditions that consider Yule to be their New Year because that is when the Sun begins a new cycle of increased light on Earth. As you learn more about the Sabbats you can determine which traditions YOU feel are most appropriate for your New Year celebration.

This Sabbat is generally celebrated on October 31st, but some traditions prefer November 1st. This is one of two "spirit-nights", the other being Beltane. Many believe it to be a magical interval when the mundane laws of time and space are temporarily suspended. It is said that when this thin veil between the worlds is lifted, it is easier to communicate with ancestors and departed loved ones as they journey through this world on their way to the Summerlands.

In Celtic countries, they would honor those who had left this world by leaving food offerings on altars and doorsteps for the "wandering dead". This was known as the "Feast of the Dead".

**Symbolism of Samhain**:
Third Harvest, the Dark Mysteries, Rebirth through Death.

**Symbols of Samhain**:
Gourds, Apples, Black Cats, Jack-O-Lanterns, Besoms

**Herbs of Samhain:**
Mugwort, Allspice, Broom, Catnip, Deadly Nightshade, Mandrake, Oak leaves, Sage and Straw

**Incense of Samhain:**
Heliotrope, Mint, Nutmeg.

**Colors of Samhain**:
Black, Orange, White, Silver, Gold.

**Stones of Samhain**:
All Black Stones, preferably jet or obsidian.

# Samhain Activities

Although most of today's Pagans are no longer country folks who grow crops and tend livestock, this can still be celebrated as a harvest, the harvest of the "thought-seeds". As the Celtic (and Witches') New Year, it's also a time for remembering the past and forecasting the future. Here are a few family-friendly activities:

## Bright Futures

Materials: 10-12 flower bulbs, A trowel or small shovel, a small spot of earth for a flower bed.

Decide where you want the flowers to bloom in the spring. Dig the holes for each bulb two and one half times the diameter of the bulb. Place or pour some fertilizer into the bottom of the hole. Place in the bulb, root side down, and cover with dirt. Water the area well. The bulbs are buried as the Sun God starts his journey to the Underworld. Just as he is not really dead, neither are the bulbs. They are warm and alive beneath the ground, in the womb of the Mother Earth, gathering strength for when they emerge next spring and bloom as bright as the Sun.

## Jack-o-Twist Lantern

Materials: 1 mini pumpkin and 1 taper candle for each "lantern" you want to make.

Cut the top off of a mini pumpkin. Make sure the opening is no larger than a quarter. Remove the seeds with a small spoon or the tip of a peeler. Allow children to paint faces on the pumpkins before sticking a taper candle into it. Carefully cut the center out of the top of the pumpkin, slightly smaller hole than in the pumpkin itself, and slip over the candle. Press the top down gently until it is a tight fit. Pagan children used turnips rather than pumpkins to make Jack-o-Lanterns, as pumpkins were not indigenous to Europe at that time.

## Natural Old Maid

For 3 or more players – children love this one!
Materials: 21 leaves, 21 index cards, glue, felt markers.

This is a two part family activity. Go outside to gather leaves a couple of days before Samhain. These leaves should not be thoroughly dried and crinkled up, but rather turning color and still pliable. Explain to your children the importance of getting the leaves from the ground rather than off the bushes or trees. Press the leaves by placing them between paper towels and stacking books on top of them. After 2 or three days, remove the leaves and select 10 pairs and one odd-one-out. Glue the leaves to the index cards, and decorate each pair as desired. Shuffle the cards and deal till all the cards are dealt. Each person picks a card from the one on their left, laying down pairs for all to see. Play continues until all pairs are matched. The person holding the odd card WINS.

## Samhain Foods & Recipes

Foods of Samhain: Turnips, Apples, Gourds, Nuts, Mulled Wines, Beef, Pork, Poultry.

### *Bewitching Apple Pancakes*
2 cups sifted all-purpose flour
2 tbs. sugar
4 tsp. baking powder
1tsp. salt
2 well beaten egg yolks
2 cups milk
2 tbs. butter/margarine, melted
1 cup finely chopped apple, peeled and cored
2 stiffly beaten egg whites
In a large non-metal bowl, sift together all the dry ingredients. In a smaller bowl, combine the milk and egg yolks. Pour mixture into the dry ingredients and stir well. Stir in the butter/margarine and apple. Fold in the egg whites. Let the batter set up for a few minutes. Cook on a hot griddle or in a large frying pan, using 1/3 cup of batter per pancake. Use a spatula or spoon to spread batter evenly. Remove from heat, dot with butter, sprinkle with powdered sugar, and roll up into log. Top with slightly heated applesauce and a dash of cinnamon. (makes 12 pancakes)

# Hallowed Stuffed Mushrooms

2- 6oz cans of broiled mushroom crowns
1 tbs. finely chopped onion
1 tsp. vegetable oil
1/4 cup smoked cheese spread
1 tbs. catsup
1/4 cup finely chopped turnip*
1 tsp. minced garlic
Fine soft bread crumbs

Drain the cans of broiled mushroom crowns. Hollow out and chop up enough of the pieces to make 3 tbs. In a sauce pan, combine the mushroom pieces, onion, turnip, and garlic. Add the vegetable oil and cook slowly over a low heat. Stir in the cheese spread and catsup. Stuff the slightly cooled mixture into the mushroom crowns and place on a greased cookie sheet. Sprinkle tops with the fine soft bread crumbs. Bake at 425 degrees for 6-8minutes.

# Winter Solstice - Yule Traditions

The date varies from December 20 to December 23 depending on the year in the Gregorian calendar. Yule is also known as the winter solstice in the northern hemisphere. In the southern hemisphere the summer solstice, or Litha, is being celebrated at this time, due to the seasonal differences.

Yule, (pronounced EWE-elle) is when the dark half of the year relinquishes to the light half. Starting the next morning at sunrise, the sun climbs just a little higher and stays a little longer in the sky each day. Known as Solstice Night, or the longest night of the year, the sun's "rebirth" was celebrated with much joy. On this night, our ancestors celebrated the rebirth of the Oak King, the Sun King, and the Giver of Life that warmed the frozen Earth. From this day forward, the days would become longer.

**Deities of Yule:**
All Newborn Gods, Sun Gods, Mother Goddesses, and Triple Goddesses. The best known would be the Dagda, and Brighid, the daughter of the Dagda. Brighid taught the smiths the arts of fire tending and the secrets of metal work. Brighid's flame, like the flame of the new light, pierces the darkness of the spirit and mind, while the Dagda's cauldron assures that Nature will always provide for all the children.

**Symbolism of Yule:**
Rebirth of the Sun, The longest night of the year, The Winter Solstice, Introspect, Planning for the Future

**Symbols of Yule:**
Yule log or small Yule log with 3 candles, evergreen boughs or wreaths, holly, mistletoe hung in doorways, gold pillar candles, baskets of clove studded fruit, a simmering pot of wassail, poinsettias, Christmas cactus.

**Herbs of Yule:**
Bayberry, blessed thistle, evergreen, frankincense holly, laurel, mistletoe, oak, pine, sage, yellow cedar

**Incense of Yule:**
Pine, cedar, bayberry, cinnamon

**Colors of Yule:**
Red, green, gold, white, silver, yellow, orange.

**Stones of Yule:**
Rubies, bloodstones, garnets, emeralds, diamonds

**Spellworkings of Yule:**
Peace, harmony, love, and increased happiness

# Yule Activities

Caroling, wassailing, burning the Yule log, decorating the Yule tree, exchanging of presents, kissing under the mistletoe, and honoring Kris Kringle the Germanic Pagan God of Yule. Below are suggested family-friendly activities:

At Yule, the Druids used to decorate their evergreen trees with images of the things they hoped the new waxing year would bring. Small fruits represented their hopes for a bountiful harvest, coins for prosperity, and charms for love and happiness. This is one of my favorite Yule traditions!

If you are decorating an evergreen tree at Yule, be sure to include symbols of your hopes and dreams for the New Year. Hang fruits or nuts that promise good health, and colorful ornaments to fill your life with beauty. Gold and silver reflect prosperity. Your tree will symbolize a beautiful world created by you and can actually help draw those things into your life in the upcoming year. If you have an outdoor tree, you can string popcorn and cranberries to ensure the birds and squirrels enjoy the seasons blessings as well.

As you celebrate the rebirth of the sun and the hope that it brings for the New Year, may you and yours experience many Yule Blessings!

NOTE: You may want to save a few branches of your Yule tree or wreath to burn on Imbolc (February 1) when you celebrate Spring's upcoming replacement of Winter.

## Yule Log Hike
Materials: Warm Clothes, Sense of Adventure.

This is an activity that can be done the weekend before Yule. On a bright crisp morning, dress warmly and head for the park, mountains, or beach. As you hike along, look for that special Yule log to place in your hearth. Ash, oak, or cedar makes great Yule logs. Try to find one that has already fallen and is on the ground. On the beach, driftwood can be found and obtained for your log.

On your way back home, look for natural decorations to adorn your Yule log with. Traditional adornments are pine cones, leaves, holly or mistletoe sprigs, rosebuds, winter flowers, wheat stalks, and corn husks. If you must cut anything from a living plant, remember to ask and thank the plant for its gift. If you don't have a fire place, select a smaller log, slightly flat on one side so that it doesn't roll. The Yule log can be set ablaze on Solstice night to help vanquish the dark and add strength to the returning sun.

## Adorning the Yule Log
Materials: Holly, Mistletoe, Rosebuds, Pine Cones, Evergreen Sprigs, Gold String/Cord, Gold Bows, Apple Cider, Flour.

After cleaning off the Yule log, you can decorate it however you chose. Children love to help with this! Glue, wire, or small holes in the log will be needed to keep the decorations in place. Once the log is decorated, "wassail" (toast and douse) it with a libation of apple cider. Finally, dust the log with white flour, set in grate in fireplace, and (parents only) set ablaze. Sometimes a part of the log was strapped to the plow the next spring to spread the blessings over the land, and another piece was saved to light the Yule log, the following year.

## *Sunny Disposition Wreath*

Materials: 1-2 Large Bundles Evergreen Boughs, 1 Bundle Holly, 1 Wreath Frame (Wire or Styrofoam), Garden Clippers, Spool of Fine Green Wire, 2 Yards Red Ribbon, Adornments.

Cut boughs into 6" to 8" pieces. Same with Holly. Cut about 20-15" pieces of the wire. Gather a bundle of boughs together, thicker at the back and fanning out in the front. Wrap wire around the bundle about 2/3 from the top. Hold bundle in place and wrap wire around the bundle and the frame. Repeat this step, only adding a sprig of holly in front. Repeat steps 1 and 2, adding holly to bundle every other time. Make sure that all the bundles face the same direction. Where the last bundle meets the bottom of the first bundle is usually barer than the rest of the wreath, so that is where you can attach a large yellow, orange, red, or gold bow to symbolize the Sun King. Now you are ready to wire on all sorts of adornments, candies, pine cones, rosebuds, seashells, small bells, or anything to make it more personal. (Tell kids about how evergreen boughs and holly were hung both inside and outside of the homes to extend an invitation to the nature sprites to join in the Yule celebration.)

## *Dough Art Decorations*

Materials: 4 cups flour, 2 cups water, 1 cup salt, Cookie Cutters, Wire Ornament Hangers, and Acrylic Paints.
Combine flour, salt, and water in a large bowl. Dough should knead easily but not be sticky, if so, add more flour. On a flat surface, lay down some waxed paper. Take a handful of the dough and roll out with a rolling pin. Cut dough into shapes with the

cookie cutters. Make a hole in top of "cookie" for wire hanger. Place on ungreased cookie sheet and put in oven at 400 degrees for 8-10 minutes or until *slightly* brown. Remove from oven and allow to cool thoroughly. Paint with acrylic paints. Allow to dry, place hanger in hole and adorn tree, packages, or hang in windows.

# Yule Foods & Recipes

Cookies and caraway cakes soaked in cider, fruits, nuts, pork dishes, turkey, eggnog, ginger tea, spiced cider, wassail, or lamb's wool (ale, sugar, nutmeg, roasted apples).

## *Yuletide Slaw*
4 cups red cabbage, shredded
1/4 cup lemon juice
1/2 teaspoon black pepper, ground
1 teaspoon salt
1/2 cup green onions, chopped
2 teaspoons sugar
1/4 cup salad oil
2 tablespoons parsley
1 green bell pepper, chopped
Combine and toss the vegetables together. Mix salt, pepper, salad oil, lemon juice, sugar and parsley and pour over the vegetable mixture. Refrigerate for 1 hour, Toss briskly before serving. Makes 8 servings.

## *Festive Ham Balls*
3 cups bisquick
2 teaspoons parsley flakes
10 1/2 cups smoked ham
2 teaspoons spicy brown mustard
4 cups sharp cheddar cheese, grated
2/3 teaspoon milk
1/2 cup Parmesan cheese

Lightly grease a 15 1/2" x 10 1/2" baking pan. Mix all above ingredients in a non-metal bowl. Shape mixture into 1" balls. Place the balls about 2" apart in the pan. Bake for 20-25 minutes at 350 degrees, or until brown. Remove from pan and serve immediately. Makes 16 servings.

## *Brighter Day Cheese Ball*

3 tablespoons finely chopped pecans
1/4 teaspoon red hot pepper sauce
1 pkg. (8-oz) Neufchatel cream cheese
1/4 teaspoon minced garlic
3 green onions w/tops, finely chopped
1 cup shredded sharp cheddar cheese
1 teaspoon Dijon mustard
1/4 cup minced parsley

Preheat the oven to 350. Spread out chopped pecans on a cookie sheet. Bake for 8 minutes or until toasted, tossing once. In a small non-metal bowl, mix the cream cheese, onions, mustard, red pepper sauce, and garlic with mixer at a medium speed for 3 minutes. Stir in the cheddar cheese. Wrap in plastic wrap and shape into approx. 4" ball, refrigerate for 15 minutes. After, on a sheet of waxed paper, toss the pecans and parsley. Unwrap the cheese ball and carefully roll it around in the mixture, covering it completely. Rewrap the cheese ball and place in refrigerator until time to serve. Serve with crackers or fresh vegetables. Makes 24 servings.

# Hot Spiced Wassail (non-alcoholic)

4 cups cranberry juice
6 cinnamon sticks
5 cups apple cider
1 orange, studded with whole cloves
1 cup water
1 apple, cored and sliced
1/2 cup brown sugar

Mix juice, cider, and water in large saucepan or crock pot. Add cinnamon sticks, clove studded orange, and apple slices. Simmer mixture for 4 hours. Serve hot. Makes 12 servings.

### Solstice Surprise Salad

1 large unpeeled cucumber
1 15 1/2 ounce can whole chestnuts
4 ounces cheddar cheese
3 tablespoons French dressing

Wash and dry cucumber. Cut into quarters, lengthwise, and then thinly slice into a non-metal bowl. Grate cheddar cheese and add to cucumber. Break up the chestnuts into fairly large pieces and add. Toss well to mix, adding the French dressing. Chill for one hour before serving. Makes 6 servings

# Imbolc Traditions

Imbolc (pronounced i-MOLK ir i-MOLG) is also called Brighid's Day. It is a Gaelic festival that is held about halfway between the winter solstice and spring equinox and marks the beginning of spring. As with all Old Tradition observances, this holiday is usually celebrated beginning at sundown on February 1 and continuing through the day of February 2. Imbolc means in the belly of the Mother because that is where seeds are beginning to stir as it is spring.

It was originally a Pagan festival associated with the goddess Brighid. This was later Christianized as a festival of Saint Brighid. Brighid was said to visit one's home at Imbolc. To receive her blessings, people would make a bed for her and leave food and drink out. Items of clothing would be left outside for her to bless. She was also invoked to protect homes and livestock.

Another name for this holiday is Oimelc, meaning milk of ewes since it is also the traditional lambing season in the old world. Herd animals have either given birth to the first offspring of the year or their wombs are swollen and the milk of life is flowing into their teats and udders.

It is the time of Blessing of the seeds and consecration of agricultural tools. It marks the center point of the dark half of the year. This holiday is especially sacred to the Celtic Fire Goddess, Brigit, patron of smithcraft, healing, midwifery, and poetry. It is the festival of the Maiden, for from this day to March 21st, it is her season to prepare for growth and renewal.

**Symbolism of Imbolc:**
Purity, Growth and Renewal, the Reunion of the Goddess and the God, Fertility and dispensing of the old to make way for the new

**Symbols of Imbolc:**
Brideo'gas, Besoms, White Flowers, Candle Wheels, Brighid's Crosses, Priapic Wands (acorn-tipped), and Ploughs

**Herbs of Imbolc:**
Angelica, Basil, Bay Laurel, Blackberry, Coltsfoot, Heather, Iris, Myrrh, Tansy, Violets, and all white or yellow flowers

**Incense of Imbolc:**
Basil, Bay, Wisteria, Cinnamon, Violet, Vanilla, Myrrh.

**Colors of Imbolc:**
White, Pink, Red, Yellow, lt. Green, Brown

**Stones of Imbolc:**
Amethyst, Bloodstone, Garnet, Ruby, Onyx, Turquoise

# Imbolc Activities

Candle Lighting (light Candles or turn on lights in each room of the house right after sunset for a few minutes to honor the Sun's rebirth), Stone Gatherings, Snow Hiking and Searching for Signs of Spring, Making of Brideo'gas and Bride's Beds, Making Priapic Wands, Decorating Ploughs, Feasting, and Bon Fires may be lit.

Doll figures of the Goddess Brighid, called a Brideo'gas (corn dollies) can be made at Imbolc. Brighid's Crosses are another good project. They can be made from wheat stalks and are symbols of protection and prosperity in the coming year.

Home hearth fires are put out and re-lit, and a besom (broom made from twigs) is place by the front door to symbolize sweeping out the old and welcoming the new. The re-birth of the Sun is honored by lighting Candles in your home.

Here are instructions for making your own Brighid doll:

## *Brideo'gas (corn dolly)*

A corn dolly would usually be made with wheat straw from the harvest. Below are directions for making a simple corn dolly.

Materials: Wheat straw, hollow straws, or raffia, some yarn or string and a small amount of cloth.

### Directions for a natural corn dolly:

If you're using real wheat straw, it should be soaked for a couple of hours before you try to bend it. If you don't have access to the real thing, the best craft material to use is raffia. It is easily found at most craft stores and resembles flattened straw.

Take about fifteen to twenty-five strands and cut it to about a foot and a half long. This will be the main body of the dolly. Fold it over in half. Where the stalks are folded is the top of your dolly's head. Take the string or yarn and tie it around the entire bundle about an inch and a half down from the top. This marks her neck.

Before you tie off her body, you'll need to make arms. Take four to six stalks and fold them over. Tie off at each end and cut the looped end so it is frayed like the other side. The frays represent her hands. Stick the arm bundle into the main bundle right under the neck, and then tie off the main bundle under the arms.

At this point the bottom of the main bundle is frayed and splayed out a bit like a skirt. This is the simplest form of corn dolly, and it can now be considered finished if all you need is a very basic doll for your purpose.

### Alternative Corn Dolly

Materials: 1-peice Wooden Clothespin, Red, Yellow, or Brown Yarn, 1 White Pipe Cleaner, Several Scraps of White Material, Black and Red Markers, Scissors, Glue, Gold Glitter.

Children will enjoy making these little Bride images that can be used later as an alter decoration. Take a scrap of white material, (silk, satin, cotton, etc.), and cut out a 6" circle. In the center of the circle cut a hole large enough to poke the "head" of the clothespin through. Fold the circle in half and cut along the fold from both perimeters to the center hole, leaving approx. 1/8 inch between each slit and center hole. Dab "neck" of clothespin with a very small amount of glue, and push clothespin "head" up through the center hole in the material. Cut appropriate length of pipe cleaner to make arms and slide up through the slit in the clothespin until it is pushed up to the end of the slits on both sides of the material. Gather the material tight around the clothespin just under the arms, and tie off with a small piece of string or yarn. Glue a couple of short pieces of yarn to the clothespin head and make eyes and mouth with markers. Finish with dabs of glue and gold glitter around the white wedding dress. A bridal veil glued to the yarn hair is optional. Explain to the children how the Goddess is a sacred bride, pure and renewed, waiting to be re-united with her consort the God.

## Imbolc Foods & Recipes

Pumpkin seeds, Sunflower seeds, Poppy seed Cakes, muffins, scones, and breads, all dairy products, Peppers, Onions, Garlic, Raisins, Spiced Wines and Herbal Teas. Traditional foods for the Imbolc celebration include those made with seeds, (to symbolize growth), raisins (a fruit of the Sun God), pork, poultry, or lamb, with sides of potatoes, cabbage, onions, and garlic. Imbolc is the mid-point of the dark half of the year, and it is a celebration of renewal and preparation for spring. Here are a few favorite recipes:

# Maiden Wakes Muffins

2 cups flour
2 Carrots, grated
1/2 cup raisins
1 green apple, peeled, cored, grated
1 cup sugar
1/2 cup almonds, sliced
2 tsp. baking soda
3 eggs
2 tsp. cinnamon
2/3 cup vegetable oil
1/2 tsp. salt
2tsp.vanilla

Soak raisins in hot water, in a covered bowl, for 30 minutes. Drain thoroughly. Preheat oven to 350 degrees. In a large non-metal bowl, mix flour, soda, cinnamon, and salt. Stir in carrots, raisins, apple, and almonds. In a separate bowl, beat eggs, oil, and vanilla until well blended. Stir the egg mixture in to the flour mixture until just wet. Grease muffin pan with a little butter or use cupcake cups. Divide the batter into the cups and bake for 20-22 minutes, or until golden brown. Cool for 5 minutes before removing from pan. This recipe makes 8 servings.

# *Returning Sun Spice Bread*

1 1/4 cup flour
1/8 cup poppy seeds
2 tsp. baking powder
3/4 cup raisins, plain or golden
1/2 tsp. baking soda
1/2 cup butter/margarine
1/2 tsp. ground ginger
3/4 cup golden corn syrup
1/2 cup light brown sugar
4 tbs. milk
1 large egg, beaten
1 tsp. mixed spices**
**Equal parts of cinnamon, nutmeg, and allspice.

Sift the flour, soda, and baking powder into a non-metal bowl. Add the mixed spice and ginger. Next add the brown sugar and raisins. Mix. Make a well in the center of the flour mixture. In a small sauce pan, melt the butter and the syrup over a low heat, and then pour liquid into the well in the middle of the flour mixture. Add the beaten egg and the milk, and mix very well. Pour into a well-greased 2-lb loaf pan and bake in a preheated oven at 325 degrees for 40-50 minutes. This bread can be made the night before as it improves with age. This recipe makes 8-10 servings.

# Spring Equinox – Ostara Traditions

Ostara or the Vernal Equinox is also known as Lady Day or Alban Eiler (Druidic). As spring reaches its midpoint around March 21, night and day stand in perfect balance, with light on the increase. The young Sun God now celebrates a hierogamy (sacred marriage) with the young Maiden Goddess, who conceives. In nine months, she will again become the Great Mother.

The Spring Equinox or Ostara is sacred to Eostre, the Saxon Goddess of Spring, Green Earth and Fertility. Ostara is said to be the Greek translation of Eostre's name. Her two symbols were the egg and the rabbit. The first Easter egg was said to have been decorated for her by a small hare determined to make the egg as beautiful and new as Eostre made the world each spring. Today her symbols are commonly known as the Easter egg and Easter bunny.

In nature, hens begin to lay eggs when there is 12 hours or more of daylight. At the onset of spring our ancestors could count on gathering fresh eggs from their chickens and the egg became a reliable symbol of rebirth in the cycle of nature.

**Herbs and Flowers:**
Daffodil, Jonquils, Woodruff, Violet, Gorse, Olive, Peony, Iris, Narcissus and all spring flowers

**Incense:**
Jasmine, Rose, Strawberry, Floral of any type

**Sacred Gemstone:**
Jasper

# Ostara Activities

Planting seeds or starting a Magical Herb Garden. Taking a long walk in nature with no intent other than reflecting on the Magic of nature and our Great Mother and her bounty

This is a wonderful time to bring a small potted herb into your home. Plants like lavender, sage or lemon balm send their fragrance through your house, reminding you that this is the time when life renews itself. A living plant helps you stay connected with nature too. Herbs are especially nice to start growing now and they will share their miraculous energies with you in the months ahead when you add them to your cooking.

Ostara traditions involving eggs include collecting eggs, decorating them, creating crafts from eggshells, gifting eggs, and burying eggs in the earth to increase the fertility of the land.

Another favorite tradition on the first day of spring is to gather wildflowers. Some people use them for magic or divination, while others collect edible flowers for feasting, or bouquets to decorate their home. Gifts of flowers are also a popular tradition.

This time of year I love to feel the new grass beneath my feet and welcome all the new life that's sprouting up around me. Vow to walk the earth in friendship, not in dominance, and enjoy every gift your Mother Earth sends your way. No matter what traditions or customs you follow, celebrate this time with joy and a thankful heart.

## Ostara Foods & Recipes

Leafy green vegetables, Dairy foods, Nuts such as Pumpkin, Sunflower and Pine, Flower Dishes and Sprouts

In short, the types of foods that are not usually available in the deep winter. Now is the time to enjoy salads, herb cakes, seed cakes and other fresh foods. To help you celebrate the season, we have included two tasty recipes below that use several of these ingredients.

## *Poppy Seed Cheese Bread*

1 cup shredded cheese
1 cup biscuit mix
1/2 cup milk
1 egg
1/4 cup chopped onions
1 TBSP poppy seeds
Combine 1/2 cheese and all biscuit mix in bowl
Add milk and stir until moistened pat dough
Combine remaining cheese, egg and onion and spread over biscuit dough. Sprinkle with poppy seeds and bake at 425 for 15 to 20 minutes.

## *Violet Salad*

1 TBSP raspberry vinegar
1 TBSP minced Shallot
1/2 tsp. Dijon mustard
Fresh ground black pepper
1 1/2 tsp. chicken stock (vegetable for vegetarians)
1 1/2 tsp. virgin olive oil
1/2 lb. mixed greens washed
1/4 cup violet blossoms
1/4 cup wild strawberries (optional)
Combine vinegar, shallot, mustard and some pepper in a small bowl. Let stand 5 minutes. Whisk in stock then oil. Toss greens with dressings, top with violets and strawberries and serve immediately.

# Beltane Traditions

Many Wiccans and Pagans celebrate Beltane. Also known as Roodmas or May Day, it is one of eight solar Sabbats. This holiday incorporates traditions from the Gaelic Bealtaine, such as the bonfire, but it bears more relation to the Germanic May Day festival, both in its significance (focusing on fertility) and its rituals (such as May pole dancing).

Some traditions celebrate this holiday on May 1 or May Day, whiles others begin their celebration the eve before or April 30th. Beltane has long been celebrated with feasts and rituals. The name means fire of Bel; Belenos being one name for the Sun God, whose coronation feast we now celebrate.

Beltane falls opposite of Samhain on the Wheel of the Year and is considered by some to be one of the most important Sabbats on the Celtic calendar. Both mark a time when the veil between other worlds is thin, where the unseen can more easily be seen. If you are living in the Southern Hemisphere, Samhain rituals are appropriate for you now.

## Beltane Activities

An early morning walk through a local park or forest could be fun for everyone. Gather up some plants or flowers to display in your home. Mom and daughter could braid their hair, and weave in a few tender blossoms.

This Sabbat is a perfect time to decorate your home with flowers and other symbols of spring. As a child, one of my favorite traditions was making May Baskets. My sisters and I would weave baskets out of paper then gather fresh flowers to fill them. On the first day of May, our mom drove us to the homes of friends and family, and we secretly hung a basket on a doorknob, or set one on the steps, to be discovered by the occupant later that morning. What a fun way to celebrate spring!

A reader wrote. "I was walking on Beltane, and I saw some wild flowers and I picked 2 of them and gave them to some friends of mine to wish them a happy Beltane. I think even doing something small like that is celebration enough, because as long as it is in your heart, the littlest gestures matter." What a great way to share the season! No matter what traditions or customs you follow, the Sabbats should be celebrated with joy and a thankful heart.

# Beltane Foods & Recipes

Breads and cereals are popular. Try oatmeal cakes sweetened with a dab of honey. Dairy foods are again appropriate.

Celebrate Beltane with ice cream, yogurt, cheese, custards, quiche or any dairy products. Oatmeal, cookies, bread and Bannock are also good.

## *Oatmeal Bread*
1 cup evaporated milk
2 TBSP vegetable oil
1TBSP vinegar
1cup all-purpose flour
1 cup firmly packed brown sugar
1tsp baking soda
1/2 tsp salt
1 cup raisins or chopped nuts
Beat milk, oil and vinegar in mixing bowl until smooth
Add oats, flour, brown sugar, baking soda and mix well
Add nuts or raisins turn into loaf pan bake at 350 for 50 - 60 minutes or until done depending on the oven.

# Summer Solstice - Litha Traditions

Midsummer, the summer solstice (June 1st), also known as Litha, is an excellent time for magic and celebration. In the past, when summer solstice drew near, our ancestors would gather herbs and flowers to use for healing or protection. They believed when the Midsummer sun reached the day of its greatest power and light, it would imbue those herbs with special magical and healing properties.

One of the most popular herbs was the plant known as 'chase-devil', which we now call St John's Wort. People used it in potions, and wove the flowers into garlands to decorate their houses or protect their farm animals. They believed that this herb could shield them from the power of evil spirits. Other herbs often used this time of year include mugwort, chamomile and lavender.

It was also a custom to light large bonfires on Midsummer Eve and stay up until midnight to welcome in Midsummer Day. If you're holding an indoor celebration, you can decorate for the Summer Solstice using any of the summer flowers and white or yellow candles can be placed on your altar.

Midsummer Night's Eve is special for adherents of the Faerie faith. Some say that fairies are most active on this night, and many believe this is a time when the future can easily be revealed. It's certainly a great time to review the first half of the year and think about what changes can be made to improve your future.

The alternative fixed calendar date of June 25 (Old Litha) is sometimes employed by Covens. The name Beltane is sometimes incorrectly assigned to this holiday by some modern traditions of Wicca, even though Beltane is the Gaelic word for May.

Litha is a perfect time for gatherings, and many celebrate the summer solstice with friends and family. However you decide to celebrate this Sabbat, I hope your summer solstice is filled with the natural magic and power that can be felt in open-air celebrations.For the northern hemisphere, the Summer Solstice or Litha is celebrated around June 21. It is also known as: Alban Heruin (Druidic). Although the name Litha is not well attested, it may come from Saxon tradition -- the opposite of Yule. On this longest day of the year, light and life are abundant. At mid-summer, the Sun God has reached the moment of his greatest strength. Seated on his greenwood throne, he is also lord of the forests, and his face is seen in church architecture peering from countless foliate masks.

**Herbs and Flowers:**
Mugwort, Vervain, Chamomile, Rose, Honeysuckle, Lily, Oak, Lavender, Ivy, Yarrow, Fern, Elder, Wild Thyme, Daisy, Carnation

**Incense:**
Lemon, Myrrh, Pine, Rose, Wisteria

**Woods Burned:**
Oak

**Sacred Gemstone:**
Emerald

# Litha Activities

If you follow the old traditions, this is an Ideal time to reaffirm your vows to the Lord and Lady or to do a dedication ritual. Litha is a Sabbat honoring the Goddess as the Mother, the God as the Father, and of their children or the child in all of us. Below are some activities to help Pagan Parents include their small children in the celebration. Head out into the back yard and enjoy the day!

## Earth Puppets

Materials: Use natural items found in the yard, tape, and glue.

The easiest kind of puppets can be made from a twig. Select a twig that forks. You now have 2 arms and a handle to hold the puppet with. Find a fallen flower, and tape the stem to the handle for the head. You can also tape the stem of a fallen leaf to the handle for the head. For clothing, wrap a leaf around the handle, and your puppet has natural summer wear.

Another puppet can be made with a pine cone. Glue the pine cone to the forked twig, for the head. Dried and fresh grass work great for hair, beards, and mustaches. Use seeds or small rocks for eyes, nose, and mouth. Make clothing out of leaves and bonnets out of flower petals or acorn caps. Use a large box or table for the stage, and enjoy the show.

## Treasure Boxes

Materials: Sturdy cardboard box, natural items for decoration, white glue, and a medium size paint brush.
This little box is for collecting "treasured" memories from summer. Start with a large shoe box and lid. Collect items from the yard, the park, and/or the beach. Glue flat items to the box, and place the non-flat items inside. To give the box a more durable finish, brush on a coat of white glue diluted with water. Children really love this project, as they see magic in these boxes and love to tell stories of where the different items came from!

# Litha Foods & Recipes

Traditional Pagan foods associated with The Litha Sabbat are fresh vegetables of all kinds and fresh fruits of yellow, orange, and red. Fresh fruit juice mixed with 7-Up compliments any meal. Since Litha is a time for the young and childlike play, the following recipes are geared towards teens preparing the meals. Here are some easy dishes that can be both fun and symbolic.

## *Sun's Up Cobbler*
1-1lb 14oz can (3 1/2 cups) halved peaches
3 slices slightly dry bread (toast on light)
1 tbs. cornstarch
1/4 cup butter or margarine, melted
1/4 tsp. salt
1/3 cup sugar
1 tbs. lemon juice
1/2 tsp. ground cinnamon
1/4 cup butter or margarine
1/4 tsp. ground nutmeg
Drain peaches, reserving 1 cup syrup. In a pan, combine cornstarch and salt and slowly blend in reserved syrup. Over med-high heat, cook and stir until mixture comes to a boil. Reduce heat and cook and stir for 2minutes. Add lemon juice, butter or margarine and peaches. Heat JUST to bubbling then pour into 10x6x11/2 inch baking dish. Cut bread lengthwise into 1 inch strips. Dip into 1/4 cup melted butter, then into mixture of sugar, cinnamon, and nutmeg. Arrange over peaches. Bake at 375 degrees for 25 minutes or until toasty. Serve with cream (optional) Makes 6 servings.

# Lunchtime Cranberry Sun Mold

2 -3oz packages orange flavored gelatin
2 7oz bottles ginger ale
1 1lb can whole cranberry sauce
2 oranges, peeled and sectioned
1 83/4 oz. crushed pineapple, undrained
1 grapefruit peeled and sectioned. In saucepan, combine gelatin and cranberry sauce. Heat and stir until almost boiling. Stir in undrained crushed pineapple and ginger ale. Remove from heat and stir until fizzing has stopped. Pour into round mold. Chill until set. Unmold onto a serving dish with a layer of lettuce leaf bedding. Garnish with orange and grapefruit sections. Top with alternating orange and grapefruit sections in a "pinwheel" array. Serve as salad or dessert.

# Lammas / Lughnasadh Traditions

At Lammas, sometimes called Lughnasadh, it's time to celebrate the first harvest of the year, and recognize that the hot summer days will soon come to an end. Celebrated July 31st - August 1$^{st}$, the plants of spring are withering and dropping their seeds to ensure future crops. Grains are ready to be harvested and the fruits are ripe for picking.

As autumn begins, the Celtic Sun God enters his old age, but is not yet dead. The God symbolically loses some of his strength as the Sun rises farther in the South each day and the nights grow longer.

The Christian religion adopted this theme and called it 'Lammas ', meaning 'loaf-mass', a time when newly baked loaves of bread are placed on the altar. An alternative date around August 5 (Old Lammas), when the sun reaches 15 degrees Leo, is sometimes used by Covens.

**Herbs and Flowers:**
All Grains, Grapes, Heather, Blackberries, Crab Apples, Pears.

**Incense:**
Aloes, Rose, Sandalwood.

**Sacred Gemstone:**
Carnelian.

## Lammas Activities

As summer passes, many Pagans celebrate this time to remember its warmth and bounty in a celebrated feast shared with family or Coven members. Save and plant the seeds from the fruits consumed during your feast or ritual. If they sprout, grow the plant or tree with love and as a symbol of your connection with the Lord and Lady. Walk through the fields and orchards or spend time along springs, creeks, rivers, ponds and lakes reflecting on the bounty and love of the Lord and Lady.

A favorite Lammas practice is to bake bread. The grain will sustain your body as you consume one of nature's sacred gifts.

Lammas is also a festival of light. You can celebrate the last long days of the year by simply lighting a yellow or white candle.

# Lammas Foods & Recipes

Traditional Foods: Apples, Grains, Breads and Berries. This Sabbat is known as the feast of bread. Meals include whole grain loafs, corn bread, berries, crab apples, barley soup and beer.

## Corn Bread

2 eggs
2 cups buttermilk
3 tbsp. shortening melted
1 1/2 tsp salt
2 1/2 cups cornmeal
1 tsp baking powder
1/2 tsp baking soda
Beat eggs, add buttermilk and melted shortening mix well
Mix dry ingredients add to egg mixture

Beat until smooth pour into greased pan\bake at 375 about 25 minutes serve hot

## Berry Parfait

Just layer strawberries then whipped cream, blueberries then whipped cream then raspberries and whip cream!

# Autumn Equinox - Mabon Traditions

Mabon, (pronounced MAY-bun, MAY-bone, MAH-boon, or MAH-bawn) is the Autumn Equinox. It is a celebration of the 2nd Harvest and usually falls around September 22nd. The Autumn Equinox divides the day and night equally. It was a time when our ancestors paid their respects to the impending dark, and gave thanks to the waning sunlight, as they stored their harvest of that year's crops.

The Druids called this celebration *Mea'n Fo'mhair* and honored the Green Man, the God of the Forest, by offering libations to trees. Today, Wiccans celebrate the aging Goddess as she passes from Mother to Crone and her consort the God as he once again prepares for death and re-birth.

*Symbolism of Mabon:*
Second Harvest, the Mysteries, Equality and Balance.

*Symbols of Mabon:*
wine, gourds, pine cones, acorns, grains, corn, apples, pomegranates, vines such as ivy, dried seeds, and horns of plenty.

*Herbs of Mabon:*
Acorn, benzoin, ferns, grains, honeysuckle, marigold, milkweed, myrrh, passionflower, rose, sage, tobacco, thistle, and vegetables

*Incense of Mabon:*
Autumn Blend-benzoin, myrrh, and sage.

*Colors of Mabon:*
Red, orange, russet, maroon, brown, and gold

*Stones of Mabon:*

Sapphire, lapis lazuli, and yellow agates

*Spellworkings of Mabon:*
This is a good time to work on protection, prosperity, security, and self-confidence. Spells for harmony and balance are also good now.

**Deities of Mabon:**
Goddesses-Modron, Morgan, Epona, Persephone and the Muses
Gods-Mabon, Thoth, Thor, Hermes, and the Green Man

# Mabon Activities

Making wine, gathering dried herbs, plants, seeds and seed pods, walking in the woods, scattering offerings in harvested fields, offering libations to trees, adorning burial sites with leaves, acorns, and pine cones to honor those who have passed over.

Mabon is considered a time of the Mysteries. It is a time to honor Aging Deities and the Spirit World. Considered a time of balance, it is when we stop and relax and enjoy the fruits of our personal harvests, whether they be from toiling in our gardens, working at our jobs, raising our families, or just coping with everyday life. May your Mabon be memorable, and your hearts and spirits be filled to overflowing!

# Mabon Foods & Recipes

Eat breads, nuts, apples, pomegranates, and vegetables such as potatoes, carrots, and onions. Offerings of ciders, wines, and herbs are appropriate at this time.

## Harvest Morning Muffins

3 eggs
1/2 cup sugar
1/2 cup vegetable oil
1 cup grated apples
1 cup grated carrots
1 cup whole-wheat flour
1 cup all-purpose flour
1 tbs. baking powder
1/4 tsp. salt
1/2 tsp. cinnamon

Preheat the oven to 375 degrees. Lightly grease a 12-muffin tin or line it with paper liners. Set aside. In the bowl blend the eggs, sugar and oil until well combined. Stir in the grated apples and carrots. In a separate bowl, sift the flours, baking powder, salt and cinnamon. Blend the dry ingredients with the apple mixture until just combined. Spoon the batter into the muffin tin and bake for 25 minutes. Makes 12 muffins

## Lunch Crumble

5 apples
1 cup rolled oats
2/3 cup brown sugar
1/2 cup all-purpose flour
6 tbs. butter
1 tsp. cinnamon
1/4 tsp. salt
1/4 tsp. allspice
2 tbs. apple juice or orange juice

Preheat the oven to 375 degrees. Lightly butter a 9-inch square baking pan or a casserole of the equivalent size, and then dust it with flour. Peel, core and slice the apples, and arrange them in the pan. In the bowl of an electric mixer, blend the oats, brown sugar, flour, butter, cinnamon, salt and allspice on low speed until it forms a coarse meal. Crumble the mixture evenly over the apple slices and sprinkle with the juice. Bake for 35 minutes. Makes 6 servings Serve warm with chilled fruit and vegetable plates, buffet style.

# Share the Wealth Applesauce

24 tart apples
Juice of a lemon
2 cups water
1 cup sugar
4 tsp. cinnamon
1 cup raisins (optional)

Peel and core the apples, then cut them into chunks. Place the apples in a large nonreactive saucepan, and add the lemon juice and water. Stir in the sugar. Bring the mixture to a boil, and then reduce the heat to low. Cover the pot and cook for 30 minutes or until the apples are soft. Remove the mixture from the heat and add the cinnamon and raisins, if desired. Stir light for a chunky sauce and rigorously for a smooth sauce. For a pink applesauce, use red apples and leave the skins on. Once the apples are soft, you can strain out the skins or lift them from the sauce with a fork.

*Makes 2 1/2 cups (Pour into resealable jars; decorate to give as Harvest gifts to relatives, friends, and neighbors.)*

# Esbats & Moon Lore

*The face of the Moon doth change its aspect, yet is ever the same;*
*. As the Holy Law doth reveal a different face to each of the*
*Children of Light, yet is unchanged in its essence.*

Essene Gospel of Peace Book #2

# Esbat Traditions

While solar activity is the basis for Sabbat celebrations, Esbats are gatherings and rituals that are traditionally scheduled around the cycles of the Moon. This is a popular time for initiation ceremonies, healing magic or other rituals that involve the lunar activity of the moon and are traditionally associated the feminine energy or the Goddess.

Lunar observance and ritual are an important part of the Wiccan religion. During an Esbat, time is usually set aside to honor the God and Goddess. However, because the Moon is a symbol of the Goddess, some traditions may focus only on the feminine aspect of the Divine. The bottom line is there is no single, preferred way to celebrate an Esbat. Let your heart guide you and do whatever you feel most comfortable with.

The cycle of the Moon has traditionally been connected with the Triple Goddess. Her three aspects include the Maiden (Crescent Moon), the Mother (Full Moon), and the Crone (Dark Moon). Two specific energy paths are also linked to the moon cycle. These are waning (decreasing) and waxing (increasing). Finally, there are thirteen Moons in a calendar year, and each is connected with a different type of energy, based on the season.

If this sounds complicated, just remember that it all boils down to simply following the increasing or decreasing energy of the moon and the natural flow of the seasons.

When it comes to the seasons, we all know that it's best to work with Mother Nature, so we plant in the spring and harvest in the fall. The same logic applies when working with the cycles of the moon. If you want to decrease, banish or remove a problem, many believe it is best to tackle that issue between the Full Moon and the

New Moon, while the moon is waning or decreasing. The day or night of the New Moon is considered the strongest for banishing. On the other hand, spells or magic for increase, growth, and gain should be done after the New Moon, while it is waxing or increasing. The day or night of the Full Moon is considered the most powerful for increasing energy work. This type of Moon magic is ancient, and it is still practiced today.

Our ancestors knew that everyone was affected by the power of the Moon and they used Her influence to better their lives. Those who practiced magic would use various lunar cycles to enhance their spells and rituals, tapping into the larger amounts of energy they believed existed during this time. The mystical influence of the Moon is still acknowledged today by most Wiccan and Pagan groups and many plan their activities around the cycles of the moon, as they feel this gives their spellwork, healing or magical rituals a little additional energy.

# Full Moon Names and Lore

In this modern world we rely on digital gadgets and calendars to help us tell time. But our ancestors used the Moon to mark time. Tracking from one Moon phase to the next allowed them to plan everything from daily activities to annual gatherings and celebrations.

There are 12 to 13 Full Moons each year, or one every 28 1/4 days. Many cultures have given names to the full moons, and different full moon names can be found among the Celtic, Old English, Native American and many other cultures. These names were based on the seasonal conditions and the activities of the people in a given area. The full moon name was used to identify the entire month during which it occurred. The names below are some of the most common, and each one tells us a lot about what life was like for the people during that time period.

### January ~ Wolf or Storm Moon
In January the stormy weather earned this moon its name. Snow covered the earth and the howling of wolves could be heard echoing through the cold winter air. Some tribes called this the Snow Moon, but that name was more commonly used for the February moon.

### February ~ Snow or Ice Moon
This moon its most common called the Snow moon, but the tribes that used this name for the January moon called this moon the Hunger Moon as the food supply was often low this time of year.

### March ~ Worm, Crow or Seed Moon
As the earth starts to warm the earthworm casts appear, inviting the return of the robins. Some tribes called this Moon the Full Crow Moon, because the cawing of crows signaled the end of winter. It was also known as the Seed Moon as it was now time for sowing.

### April ~ Hare or Pink Moon

The Hare was a sacred animal associated in Roman legends with springtime and fertility. In other areas, this moon was known as the Pink Moon, named after the flowers that began to appear, including the widespread grass pink or wild ground phlox. Other variations indicate more signs of full spring, such as Sprouting Grass Moon, Egg Moon, and Fish Moon (common among coastal tribes).

### May ~ Flower, Milk or Dyad Moon

Flowers come into full bloom and corn is ready to plant. It is also called the Corn Planting Moon and the Milk Moon. Some call it the Dyad moon, (the Latin word for a pair). This refers to the twin stars of the constellation of Castor and Pollux.

### June ~ Mead or Strawberry Moon

During late June and most of July the meadows, or meads, were mowed for hay. This moon is also called the Strawberry Moon, as Strawberry picking season reaches its peak during this time. This is one of the few names that were universal to all Algonquin tribes.

### July ~ Wort, Hay or Buck Moon

When the sun was in Leo, the worts (from the Anglo-Saxon wyrt plant) were gathered to be dried and stored. Some tribes also called it the Hay Moon Perhaps most commonly known as the Buck Moon, because deer start growing velvety hair-covered antlers in July.

### August ~ Sturgeon or Barley Moon

Sturgeon, were most readily caught during this month. A few tribes called it the Full Red Moon because, as the Moon rose, it appeared reddish through any sultry haze. It was also called the Green Corn Moon or Grain Moon. Persephone, virgin Goddess of rebirth, carries a sheaf of barley as a symbol of the harvest.

### September ~ Corn or Harvest Moon

The September full moon is actually the Harvest Moon, which is the full Moon that occurs closest to the Autumn Equinox. In two years out of three, the Harvest Moon comes in September, but in some years it occurs in October. Native Americans sometimes refer to it as the Corn moon because it marked the time when corn was supposed to be harvested. The chief Indian staples of corn, pumpkins, squash, beans, and wild rice are now ready for gathering.

## October ~ Blood or Hunter's Moon

Native Americans named this moon the Full Hunter's Moon or Blood Moon as it was now time to begin storing up meat for the long winter ahead. Leaves are falling and hunters can easily see the animals they hunt. The Hunter's Moon is historically an important feast day in both Western Europe and among many Native American tribes.

## November ~ Beaver or Oak Moon

Beavers were actively preparing for winter and they provided a source of warm winter furs for trappers. This moon is sometimes also referred to as the Frosty Moon. Others call it the Oak Moon, named after the sacred tree of the Druids which withstands winter storms.

## December ~ Cold or Long Night Moon

As Winter arrives the temperatures plummet. Some also call this the Long Night Moon as the nights lengthen and the moon spends more time above the horizon.

## The Blue Moon ~ Variable

A Blue Moon occurs when the moon with its 28 day cycle appears twice within the same calendar month. Many consider the Blue Moon to be a goal moon where you set specific goals for yourself.

## The Black Moon ~ Variable

A Black Moon occurs when there are two dark cycles of the moon in any given calendar month. It is believed that the second dark moon is a time of great power within the spiritual world and any magic worked during this time is especially powerful.

## Esbat Rituals

In Wicca, Esbat rituals are ceremonies that celebrate and strengthen our connection with the Goddess, the God and the Earth. Both Sabbats and Esbats are times of real, as well as symbolic power. These rituals will vary greatly, but all relate to the Goddess (Moon) and God (Sun) and to our home, the Earth. By observing the Sabbats and Esbats, Wiccans attune themselves to the Earth and reaffirm their Earth roots. Embrace the magic of these days and nights, and celebrate them every chance you get!

# Personalizing Your Path

## *Choosing Your Sabbat & Esbat Activities*

At this point, you've learned a lot about Sabbats and Esbats, but you may still be wondering exactly what activities are best for YOU on these magical days and nights. If you talk to a dozen practitioners and read all the best-selling books on this subject, you will likely discover that there are just as many different rituals for these occasions as there are practioners. Do you choose the oldest, or the most popular, or is it acceptable to create new rituals, unique to your personal practice? How do you know which is best?

In Wicca, rituals are intended to be ceremonies that celebrate and strengthen our connection with the Goddess, the God and the Earth. If using someone else's ritual allows you to feel more confident in the results, then you should feel free to do so. Using an established or formal ritual can also eliminate some of the work and make the event a little easier. This can be helpful when you are just getting started.

However, there are a few things to consider when using traditional rituals. First, it is not the spoken words or activities in a ritual that inspire magic. It's the power of your thoughts and the depth of the feelings evoked by the rituals that are important. If the words in a ritual do not come from your heart, they simply will not have the same power as those that do.

Second, the more energy you put into a ritual, the more likely you are to get the results you want. Borrowing someone else's ritual means you are putting some of THEIR energy into your celebration, so you may want to at least add your own personal touch to it whenever you can.

Finally, if a ritual written by another calls for specific candles, oils or items you do not have, don't hesitate to improvise or modify as needed. Again, the Divine will not ignore you simply because your candle is not the recommended green color or you are burning a different kind of oil.

The tools you use are simply intended to influence your personal thoughts and feelings. The Universe responds to the ENERGY you are sending out, so you don't want to be expressing any negative thoughts of concern. Keep your focus on the purpose or your ritual and always communicate with a heart full of joy and gratitude!

## *Using Your Own Rituals*

One of the best ways to learn Wicca is to practice it using rituals you've written yourself. This can strengthen your personal connection with the Deities and help you understand the true nature of the path. Your rituals don't have to be traditional, pre-planned or rehearsed. Many Wiccans feel that spontaneous, informal rituals can be extremely effective.

A ritual can be as simple as a solitary practitioner lighting a candle under the light of a full moon, or just sitting quietly in the grass under a shady tree on a hot day. It doesn't matter if the words of a ritual are ancient or newly inspired, as long as they create an awareness of the deities in the mind and heart of the practitioner.

If you want to practice Wicca, allowing the spirit of the moment and the wisdom of the Divine to fill you with inspiration is a wonderful way to honor the Deities. You can time your rituals to coincide with the seasons, Pagan holidays, phases of the Moon or any other days you feel particularly attracted to. But whatever you choose to do, make sure you do it in the spirit of joy and gratitude. This opens your heart and allows the bountiful gifts of the Divine to start flowing freely into your life.

If you're not celebrating the Sabbats or Full Moon Esbats because you haven't been initiated yet, don't think you have the right tools, or you're waiting for a teacher to show you how, set those excuses aside. The God and Goddess will accept you just the way you are, on any day of the year, and they certainly don't REQUIRE you to use special tools, candles, herbs or oils in your communication with them.

To truly connect with the Deities, make sure your words and actions always express YOUR OWN thoughts and feelings. Use tools if you find them helpful, but understand that the Divine in not in your tools. These objects can only help you focus your mind and draw out the Divine power that already resides within you.

You are now ready for simple celebrations and rituals. In his best-selling book Wicca: A Guide for the Solitary Practitioner, Scott Cunningham tells us *"The presence of like-minded people is wonderful, but can be inhibiting as well. There are certainly rituals at which others can't be present. An unexpected glimpse of the Full Moon half-shrouded in clouds calls for a few moments of silence or attunement, an invocation, or meditation. These are all rituals shared with the Goddess and God alone. Deities don't stand on ceremony; they're as unpredictable and flowing as Nature Herself."*

Rituals like those mentioned above are my favorite kind, and they are ones you can experience daily. Look for opportunities to greet the God and Goddess everywhere you go. Remember to keep your rituals simple. Get outside and feel the cool earth beneath your feet, enjoy the fresh air and listen to the sounds of the wind as it slips through the leaves. Your Mother Earth has many magical gifts to share with you.

*"With the eyes and ears of the spirit do you see and hear the sights and sounds of the kingdom of the Earthly Mother: the blue sky where dwells the angel of Air, the clear river where flows the angel of Water, the golden light which streams from the angel of Sun. And I tell you truly, all these are within you as well as without; for your breath, your blood, the fire of life within you, all are one with the Earthly Mother."*

*Excerpt from The Essene Gospel of Peace Book 4*

# PART 2 : A BEGINNER'S GUIDE

# TO EARTH MAGIC

## *Working With Magic*

As you find your connection to the Earth and all that is natural, and alive in the universe, your life will take on a magical air. Magic begins to flow as you live in balance with the rhythms of nature and know that you are a vital force within that flow.

**You will find Magic everywhere!**

*"In everything that is life is the law written. You find it in the grass, in the tree, in the river, in the mountain, in the birds of heaven, in the fishes of the sea; but seek it chiefly in yourselves."* Excerpt from an ancient manuscript, The Teachings of the Elect

Wicca, like most spiritual paths, teaches that the Divine is within us and in everything around us. You are a part of this supreme universal power and MAGIC IS ALREADY WITHIN YOU!

What you imagine, you have the power to create! With magic you can create your dreams, heal your world, love your life and find the peace that lives in every human heart.

**Are you ready to start living a magical life?**

## *Generating Positive Magic*

You were meant to live a magical life. While it may not as be as simple as waving a magic wand and saying a few special words, the process is not as complicated or mysterious as many people believe.

Wiccans and Pagans know that Divine energy exists in all things. It's in plants, stones, colors, sounds, movements, words, and it is continually flowing through our lives every day.

Earth Magic is natural magic and it is at work all around you whether you choose to formally "practice" it or not. When you learn how it works, it can help you draw more positive energy into your life and allow you to shield yourself from some of the negative energy.

This process is natural, not supernatural, and we all have the ability to direct the flow of this energy. Getting the outcome you desire is primarily a matter of training your mind.

Have you ever focused your thoughts on a goal and verbalized what you needed or wanted, only to be disappointed when nothing happened? You may have been sending out mixed messages. For example, at some point in our lives, most of us have sent forth words or thoughts that we wanted better health or money to pay bills. What we were actually *feeling* at the time was ill or broke!

If what you are thinking and feeling are not in sync, how you truly FEEL will always decide the outcome. By visualizing in your mind what it feels like to have vibrant health or to pay your bills in full, you are *sending forth the actual type of energy you want returned* to you. It's essential that both your thoughts AND feelings reflect what you want to draw into your life.

You can change the type of energy that is flowing into your life by simply changing the energy you are sending out into the world. Okay, maybe this is not always a "simple" thing to do, but it is essential if you want to start living life at its fullest. No magical ritual or spell will ever work properly for you if you don't sync your thoughts and feelings first.

Whenever you complain about your job, lack of funds, low energy or poor treatment you have received, the frustration you send out into the world will draw more things back into your life to complain about.

On the other hand, when you start finding things to be grateful for, the Universe responds quickly by filling your life with more things to be thankful for. Start with little things. Be thankful for the hot cup of coffee you had time for in the morning. Be thankful for catching the bus to work or finding a parking space right in front of the store. Be thankful that you have a job or the days you have off. Be thankful for the meal you share with family or friends. There is no shortage of things to be thankful for.

Start today and put this Universal power to the test by sending out only the type of energy you want multiplied. As you begin to experience new blessings you'll come to understand that the power to change your world has always been inside you and you'll be well on your way to living a magical life!

## Avoiding Negative Magic

Thanks in part to popular movies on witchcraft and misguided superstitions that are still being spread today, some believe that magic is only possessed by "chosen" ones. Others have concluded that Magic is evil and should not be tampered with. Neither of these statements are accurate.

Magic is a natural energy or power. It is already within you and in everything around you. By learning how to draw on this natural energy in a positive way, you can bring about incredible change in your life.

When magic gets portrayed as a supernatural force or power, it causes concern that if a mistake is made or something is done wrong, bad things can happen. It is important to understand that we are not talking about a supernatural power, but rather a natural energy that is already within you and in everything around you. It responds to ALL your thoughts and feelings whether you want it to or not.

By controlling the type of energy (thoughts and feelings) you send forth into the world, you control the type of energy that flows back into your life.

Understanding and obeying this Universal Law is the first step to achieving the life you have always dreamed about. In Wicca, this is known as the Law of Three or the Three-fold Law. A line from the Wiccan Rede gives us this wise advice:

*"Mind the Three-fold Laws you should, three times bad and three times good."*

Today, most of us know this as the Universal Law of Attraction. It's simply a reminder that whatever type of energy you send forth into the Universe will tend to come back to you three-fold!

The Rede concludes with the line:

### *"An Ye Harm None, Do What Ye Will"*

Keep this in mind and practice responsibly. Be aware that if you try to use Magic to influence or control others in any way, it can result in that type of energy returning three-fold. You can best protect yourself from drawing unwanted negative energy into your life by not sending any out!

*I cannot stress enough that you should only send forth the type of thoughts and feelings you want to multiply in your life.*

**Tips to Remember:** If the magic in your life is not working the way you want it to, focus on changing the type of energy you are sending out. Make sure your thoughts and feelings are in sync so that your message is clear, and if they are not, know that the FEELINGS you send out will ultimately determine what the Universe returns to you.

## Developing a Magical Mind

*"Do not think because it cannot be seen, that thought has no power. I tell you truly, the lightning that cleaves the mighty oak, or the quaking that opens up cracks in the earth, these are as the play of children compared with the power of thought."*

(Excerpt from an ancient manuscript called the Teachings of the Elect)

In part 2 of this book, we will cover the traditional tools used in rituals and spells. While these tools can certainly influence magical power, for the most part, it's the user who gives them their power, and not the other way around. You already have within you the ability to create a magical life for yourself and your MIND is your most powerful magical tool!

***"All that we are is a result of what we have thought."*** Buddha

But conditioning your mind to always generate the proper signals can be challenging. As you worry about the bills you need to pay, a health issue or a relationship that is not exactly what you want, the Universe is faithfully responding by sending you more of what you are focused on.

If you want to change your circumstances, you must first change your thinking. Start each day by expressing your gratitude for all the little blessings in your life and you will soon discover you have much more to be grateful for.

Since the Universe does not communicate with us through mere words, your words or thoughts will need to inspire intense feelings within you for them to be effective. When your thoughts and feelings are in sync, this sends a clear message to the Universe.

Imagine in your mind what it would actually FEEL like to have what you desire and express your sincere gratitude to the Goddess and God for sending you these things. When the images in your mind are clear enough to generate the feeling of vibrant health, happiness, peace or whatever it is you are seeking, you will begin to draw more of these things into your life.

If you're not getting the results you want, take a closer look at ALL your thoughts and feelings. Are you expressing gratitude for the blessings in your life, or are you complaining about lack of money, low energy or the negative energy others are sending your way? You are in complete control of the thoughts and feelings you send out. Make sure they are what you want to see multiplied in your life.

As is recorded in the Blue Book of our forefathers, **true Magic is *'The art and science of changing states of mind at will."***

This is why I encourage individuals to create their own magic rituals and spells. You will experience the best results if what you desire comes from your heart. Don't simply utter words or mimic the actions of another person. Let the Divine know how YOU feel about an issue or event.

## A Simple Magic Exercise

Here is a simple magical technique you may wish to try. To help you achieve your goal (magical or otherwise), find a word or short phase which sums up what it is that you want to accomplish. Write the word (or phrase) down 10 times each day until you achieve success.

## *Creating Sacred Space*

Magical energy is everywhere, but its flow can be altered, or even unknowingly blocked by thoughts or surroundings. Having a special area that you can retreat to, whether inside or outdoors, can make a big difference when it comes to your magical energy. If magic does not seem to be working for you as it should, you can encourage it to flow freely again with a few simple changes in your surroundings.

A good place to start is in your home. There is an old proverb that suggests "home is where the heart is" and because magic always comes from the heart, your home should be considered a natural source of magic. At the very least, it's a sacred and powerful place with a roof and walls that shield you from the elements. The door protects those within from unwanted intrusions. You may not be able to control what goes on outside your home, but within its walls, you have some freedom to create the world you want to live in.

Your home, or at least some small area within it, should give you a feeling of comfort and peace when you enter, no matter how chaotic the day's work or family life has been. You can create beauty, enchantment and natural magic in your home by bringing a little of nature indoors.

Change the energy of a room with seasonal decorations. Use sweet-smelling flowers in Spring, bowls of fresh fruit or herbs in the Summer, set out pumpkins and colored leaves in Autumn or baskets of pinecones and evergreen branches in Winter. These symbols of the season are beautiful and usually inexpensive or free.

The wise Wiccan will follow nature's cue and use natural decor in their home to accent each season. This brings magical energies into the home and helps reconnect those within to the energies of the natural world.

NOTE: It's always best to decorate with live plants, as they can bring a healthy energy and vibration to your home, but silk plants or even prints and artwork of the outdoors can also help the mind connect with nature. If you decide to use artificial greenery, try to have at least one potted plant in the mix.

Small water fountains, or even bubbling fish tanks are nice additions too, as they provide the soothing sound of running water and bring the magical energies of water into your home. DVD's of nature sounds can also create a relaxing atmosphere.

If you grow flowers or herbs, you can bring in fresh cut roses, lavender, or sage to hang in your kitchen. Their aromas can invoke the element of air.

For the element of earth, simply gather an assortment of pebbles, or set out your collection of stones and crystals in a ceramic bowl.

Lighting candles would add the element of fire, bringing all four elements into the room.

These are all small things, but they can have a big impact on your energy level and peace of mind... and THAT will have an influence on the flow of magical energies in your life.

When the weather permits, open a door or window to invite in fresh air. The magical energies of Air can also be influenced with aromatherapy. This power is something that many of us overlook in our busy lives, but it has long been used to influence our mood.

When we enter our home the first thing that greets us is the aroma. Essential oils like sweet orange and clove spice can be used to create a warm refreshing atmosphere on cold dreary winter day. Aromas can help lift our spirit and will encourage family and friends to relax and linger in a cozy, inviting atmosphere.

Candles fragranced with essential oil can be used to give your home a pleasant ambience and aroma. You can also add 6-8 drops of your favorite scent to water in a diffuser or simply place the drops directly into a bowl of boiling water. If you place a drop or two of oil on a cold light bulb, the fragrance will fill the room as the bulb warms up. Three or four drops of your favorite essential oil on a cotton ball can add a hint of fragrance to a drawer or cupboard in your home.

NOTE: You can read more on the use of herbal, crystal and candle magic in Book #3 of the Living Wicca Today Series, *Wicca: A Beginner's Guide to Casting Spells.*

Finally, we highly recommend that you allow your Mother Earth to bless your kitchen with an assortment of unprocessed foods. Her bountiful gifts of living foods can help improve your health and increase your lifespan. Spiritual leaders from many different paths also believe that these foods actually enhance our ability to communicate with the Divine.

The bottom line is, the more ways you find to connect with Nature, the more opportunities the Divine has to offer you wisdom, healing and true spiritual fulfillment!

Many of these tips can also be used to generate magical energy in your office at work or even in your car to make your commuting more enjoyable.

Today, look for simple ways to bring the beauty of Nature into your home. Start with one room, or even a corner in a room, and build a magical atmosphere that will create a feeling of comfort, peace and happiness when you enter the space. This will help the magical energies to flow freely through your life.

## Your Altar

Your altar is a place of power and magic. It's also a place for you to express your faith and to do your spiritual or magical work. Some Wiccans maintain an altar as a decorative space in their home or garden, but most will set it up and dismantled it for each ritual.

You may want to have a round altar to represent the Goddess, or you might prefer a square one that is symbolic of the elements. Either is fine. It can be set up on any flat surface. A small table is nice, but even a cardboard box will work in a pinch.

If you are outdoors, you can use any available flat space, including the ground, a log, a stump, or a large rock. During outdoor rituals a fire is sometimes used for the altar.

The exact layout is a matter of personal preference. Use your imagination when setting up your altar. If you don't have all the traditional items, use a nature-based altar plan. A round stone might represent the Goddess, or a seashell can work in place of a cup or chalice, and a small branch makes a wonderful wand to represent the God.

Tools sacred to the Goddess, like the cup or cauldron, are usually placed on the left, while symbols of the God, such as the wand or athame, are placed on the right. Flowers and the censer are commonly placed in the center so the aroma and smoke can be offered up to both Deities. In some traditions the altar is set up facing North which is associated with the Earth, but others prefer to set it up facing East, where the Sun and Moon rise.

Don't get so wrapped up in the details of setting up your altar that you miss the joy of celebration with the Goddess and God. These are simply traditions. As far as the Deities are concerned, there is no right or wrong way to commune with them. They welcome all with open arms.

An altar can be simple, perhaps holding only a flower and a candle on a small stump outside. Or it can be elaborate, with a full size table, a special altar cloth, candles, ritual tools, incense, herbs or flowers, and statues of their God and Goddess. The choice is yours.

In his book, Wicca: A Guide for the Solitary Practitioner, Scott Cunningham describes the Wiccan altar and ritual this way: *"Though we may setup images of the Goddess and God, we're not idol worshippers. We don't believe that a given statue or pile of rocks actually is the deity represented. And although we reverence nature, we don't worship trees or birds or stones. We simply delight in seeing them as manifestations of the universal creative forces-the Goddess and God. The altar and the magic circle in which it stands is a personal construction and it should be pleasing to you."*

I believe that when we feel happy inside, the Divine is happy too!

## Your Magical Tools

Tools can be helpful in creating a magical life. In Wicca, certain objects are traditionally used in ritual to help invoke the Deities, banish negativity, or direct energy. Your Craft tools can help you create the proper frame of mind or atmosphere for your magical work. They don't need to be elaborate, but they should be special to you.

To better understand the role your tools play, think back to a time when you dressed up for a job interview or an important social event. What you wore made you feel better about yourself, and thus improved your chances for a successful outcome. You knew that your clothes didn't really have magical powers, but there was no question that having the right outfit and accessories boosted your self-confidence, and THAT is why these things are important. Magical tools work the same way. They are a part of our rituals because they can help us focus our thoughts and generate the ideal atmosphere to work in.

Below you will find a list of the most common tools and their general uses. While these items are not required to practice Wicca, you may want to collect some of them to enrich your rituals. You can shop for these tools in our Magical Store, or search through antique and second-hand shops for them. Some prefer to make their tools and infuse them with a little of their own energy.

In addition to the standard tools like the athame, cauldron or broom, use tools such as relaxing nature sounds and music, fragrance or aromatherapy, and candles, stones, pendants or even wands, to help you focus your thoughts. Just remember, these are ONLY tools, and not the real source of your power.

# Common Craft Tools

**Athame**: A ritual blade, usually double edged, with a black or dark handle. The two sides symbolize the God and the Goddess, coming together at the point to join the spiritual and mundane worlds. It is never used to cut anything on the physical plane. This tool is only used to direct energy that is raised during rites and spells. It is most often associated with the element of air and the east quarter, but some associate it with fire and the south. Coven members can share many of the ritual tools, but the athame is always personal. The sword is a larger version of the ritual knife or athame, and stories of magical swords seem to be quite common in mythic literature!

**Bells**: Often used to invoke directional energies, to ring in the sunrise on a Sabbat, or to invoke the Goddess in ritual. Some believe they can be rung to ward off evil spells and spirits, and many others use them to evoke good energies or bring good luck. You can place them in cupboards or hang them on a door to guard your home, or ring them in ritual to signal a spell's beginning or end. Any type of bell can be used.

**Besom**: A witch's broom is still used in Wicca today. Some begin rituals by sweeping the energy out of the circle space (indoors or out) before drawing the circle. The bristles do not need to touch the ground. While brushing, simply visualize the broom sweeping the area to purify it for your ritual workings. The broom was traditionally thought to be a powerful tool against curses and practitioners of evil magic. Some believed that laying a broom across the doorway could block any spells sent to the house or to those in it. Some also use the broom to raise energy in a circle. The broom is most often associated with earth and the north, but some traditions link it to air and the east.

**Book of Shadows**: Also called a BOS, is a witch's book of spells, rituals and magical lore. It's your personal magical journal and can be one of your most valuable tools.

**Boline or Bolline**: A white-handled knife used in magic or ritual. Unlike the Athame, which is only used in ritual, this is a working knife. It may be used to cut wands, cords, sacred herbs, flowers, or to inscribe symbols onto wood, candles or wax.

**Candles**: Candles are used at most all Wiccan rituals and celebrations. You can place candles on the altar to represent the God and Goddess, to mark the quarters, or simply to help set the mood for something magical. We suggest you keep a good supply on hand at all times. Candles represent fire and the south.

**Cauldron**: This tool symbolizes the Goddess or feminine aspect of the Divine and the waters of rebirth. The cauldron is an ancient vessel used for cooking and brew making. It is the container in which magical transformations take place. It is also symbolic of the element of Water. Celtic legends about Kerridwen's cauldron have influenced some Wiccan traditions. The cauldron can also be used as a tool for scrying (gazing) if you fill it with water and stare down into its depths.

**Chalice or Cup**: A ritual tool, the chalice represents the female principals of creation. It is used to drink from, especially in rituals where feminine symbolism is important. The chalice can be made from most anything. Feel free to use one made from glass, ceramic, wood or metal. The chalice is most often associated with water and the west.

**Crystal Sphere**: The quartz crystal sphere has been used in Divination since ancient times. Most crystal balls on the market today are glass or plastic. Genuine quartz crystal spheres can be determined by their inclusions or irregularities. Larger crystals are beyond most budgets, as they often retail for several hundred dollars. Small crystals can be effective too. The diviner simply gazes into the ball until images appear in the mind or in the depths of the crystal, revealing the information they are seeking. Some use the crystal ball at Full Moon rituals, and believe that exposure to moonlight can increase its ability to inspire our psychic powers.

**Grimoire**: A magical workbook containing ritual information, magical properties of natural objects and preparation of ritual equipment. Often used interchangeably with Book of Shadows.

**Incense**: You can burn herbs, oils, or other aromatic items to scent the air during acts of magic and ritual. Incense purifies the ritual space and you can consecrate items being used in ritual by passing them through the smoke. Any type of incense and censer (burner) can be used in a Wiccan ritual. The incense represents fire and air, as well as south and east.

**Pentacle**: A circle surrounding a five-pointed, upright star (pentagram). Worn as a symbol of a witch's beliefs. The five points represent the Earth, Air, Fire, Water and Spirit. This symbol is often worn as a pendant or placed on the Wiccan altar. Some also hang Pentacles over doors and windows to provide protection for those within.

**Wand:** The wand has been used for thousands of years in both magic and religious rites. This tool is often used to invoke the Goddess and God. It is also used to direct energy, to draw magical symbols on the ground, or even to stir brew in a cauldron. For some Wiccans it represents the element of Air and it's a symbol of the God or masculine aspect of the Divine.

The length and type of wood vary by tradition, so feel free to cut yours as long or as short as you like. You may also want to strip the bark or carve magical symbols into your wand. The choice is yours.

**NOTE**: At the end of this book I have listed a glossary of additional Wicca and Witchcraft terms and their definitions. I hope you will find this reference helpful as you continue your studies.

**TIP**: Don't be too concerned if you lack the proper candles, aromas or other suggested tools for magical work, Focus on sending out positive thoughts and feelings. The words you utter or the tools you use in your magical rituals, will not affect the results nearly as much as the actual thoughts and feelings you send forth into the Universe.

You won't fail at magic because you used the wrong color candle or different incense than suggested. Always remember that wands, candles, oils and other items are simply used to help you focus your thoughts and set the mood for magical activities.

*"My brother, tree! Let me not hide myself from thee, but let us share the breath of life which our Earthly Mother hath given to us.*

*More beautiful than the finest jewel of the rug maker's art, is the carpet of green leaves under my bare feet; More majestic than the silken canopy of the rich merchant, is the tent of branches above my head, through which the bright stars give light."*

Essene Gospel of Peace Book 2

# Increasing Your Magical Energy

No matter what path we choose to walk, Mother Earth has an effect on our lives. We have all been refreshed by the feel of soft grass beneath our feet, the fresh outdoor air and the warmth of the sun on our face or the cool waters of a lake or stream.

*"Always have the Brothers of Light lived where rejoice the angels of the Earthly Mother: near rivers, near trees, near flowers, near the music of birds; where sun and rain may embrace the body, which is the temple of the spirit."* The Teachings of the Elect

Most are satisfied with this natural exchange of energy, and they will go outdoors to recharge whenever they find time to. But in Wicca, you can learn methods to draw on and amplify this Divine energy whenever you need it.

As you learn how to work with this energy, always be respectful of the powers and spirits of our Mother Earth. You are not trying to control the forces of nature and bend them to your will. You are simply working WITH them to influence the direction they flow through your life.

If you are raising energy for spellwork or magical purposes, you know how important it is to follow the Harm None rule and remember the Three-fold Law. To consistently insure the best results, you may also want to focus your work on what you can GIVE to the Earth and those around you.

As the three-fold law teaches, the more positive energy you send out, the more you get back. You simply can't out-give the Universe. Thoughts and energy sent forth from a giving or loving heart will always multiply and return to you in kind.

On the other hand, if you allow your mind to simply focus on what you need or want, you may end up multiplying your needs and wants. This is why many get discouraged with spellwork and magic. They send forth the wrong type of thoughts and energy and then wonder why the results were not what they expected. *Keep in mind that anytime you worry about negative or harmful energies, you give them added power.* If you worry too much, you can actually draw more negative energy into your life.

So, as you begin any energy work, if you want positive results, always make sure you are sending forth positive thoughts AND feelings. Fill your mind with peaceful and relaxing images. Imagine what it feels like to already have the results you desire. Without clear, positive thoughts that generate positive feelings, negative energies can easily slip in and affect your results.

Finally, don't expect magical results to happen overnight. With a strong will and solid visualization skills, you can achieve what others believe is impossible. But, as with the muscles in your physical body, the strength of your thoughts or mind must be developed over time.

It will take practice. The more you exercise your visualization skills, the stronger your mind becomes. The stronger your mind or intent is, the more effective your magic will be. Some will find it easier than others, but ALL are capable of developing these skills!

# Grounding

The thoughts that you hold in your mind have a significant impact on what you will experience during magical work. Each day, your thoughts and actions are affected by the energy of the places you go and the people you see. It's always a good idea to clear any negative beliefs or feelings you may be holding about yourself and others before you begin ritual or spellwork. Grounding is a great way to remove negativity and excess energy from your mind and body.

In Wicca, grounding can be described as the process of getting rid of negative or excess energy by pouring it into the Earth (the ground). The Earth is a great purifier. You can then draw energy back out of the ground to renew yourself. The energy you draw from it is clean energy. By taking some of her energy, you make yourself more like your Mother Earth, and your connection can help you become stronger, more focused and calm.

One popular method of grounding is to imagine you are a tree. Visualize roots extending from your feet into the ground, then allow all negative energy to flow out through your roots. When you have released your negative thoughts and feelings into the ground, then draw fresh energy in just like a tree would draw in water.

Some prefer to sit on the ground and place their hands on the Earth as they imagine roots extending from their fingertips into the ground. You can also literally hug a tree. The strength of the tree connects you to the Earth and allows you to release your energy into it where it can flow down the tree into the earth.

Just remember to draw clean, fresh energy back into yourself after you ground your old energy. If you forget to reset your energy levels you may simply feel drained.

Another tradition suggests that you pick up a stone and release your negative energies into it, then toss it into a lake or pool of water where the unwanted energy can be washed away. Some have found that a simple bath or shower works to wash away stress and help them ground.

Many different methods work well for releasing negative energies. Most will involve a bit of visualization to clear the mind. How well a method works for you will depend on how easy it is for you to visualize the results. You may need to experiment to find what works best for you.

A passage from a 2000 year old manuscript records several Essenes men kneeling at a tree they believed the life-force or energy of the Divine flowed through. It's a beautiful image.

*"...there he knelt at the place where the roots, gnarled and hoary with age, spread over the river edge. And the Sons of Light knelt also, and they did touch with reverence the trunk of the ancient tree, for it was taught to them that the trees are the Brothers of the Sons of Men. For their mother is the same, the Earthly Mother, whose blood runs in the sap of the tree and in the body of the Son of Man."*

## Raising Energy

In Wicca, energy and nature are one. Mother Earth can help you renew your energy when you become attuned to nature. Divine energy naturally flows through everything. It connects us to each other and to the world we live in. This energy can be directed by your thoughts, feelings and activities, so it's important to learn exactly what increases or drains it.

Your mind simply needs to visualize or sense the Earth and it will naturally begin to draw energy from the connection you have to her. Sometimes this may only take a few short minutes. However, when life is extra tough, or if the actions of others seem to be draining your energy, you may need prolonged or multiple sessions to truly refresh your spirit.

Reach out as much as you need to. Your own spirit must be strong if you hope to banish the unwanted spirits or negative energies in your life.

The Divine has always existed in Nature and always will. You can count on Mother Earth to be there for you, waiting to lift your spirit and comfort you. Her Divine energy is far stronger than that of any individual, and if you stay connected to her, she will help you find the strength to face all conflicts or challenges in your life.

The methods you use to raise energy are similar to those used to ground it. You can amplify your energy by visualizing it entering your body as you draw it from the Earth.

Some see themselves as a tree drawing energy from the ground. Others imagine her energy entering and flowing through their body as they drink a glass of water or juice.

Whenever I consume fresh fruit, I think about the life-energy of the living food entering my body and merging with my own. Spiritual leaders from many different paths also believe that living foods (fresh fruits and vegetables) actually enhance our ability to communicate with the Divine. If this is true, then consuming Mother Earth's living foods can help raise both physical and spiritual energy.

No single method works for everyone. Use whatever combination of methods you are most comfortable with to draw energy from the Earth. As you send forth your intentions in rituals and magical work, don't forget to give back to the Earth and those around you, and always be thankful for strength and power given to you.

## *Casting Circles*

In Wicca, the circle is used to create a sacred space in which we can welcome and honor the Goddess and God. Rituals and magical workings usually take place within such a circle. While other religions use a building such as a church or temple to hold worship, Wiccans and Pagans can cast a circle any place they choose.

In ancient times, some of our ancestors worshiped in stone circles, while others met in sacred groves or meadows. At the point in history when Pagan rites were outlawed, most practioners grew secretive about their rituals. Some began to practice only under the cover of darkness. Others began practicing indoors. Wicca has inherited these traditions. Many today still practice indoors, and while that is acceptable, it's ideal to hold the rites outside whenever possible, surrounded by Nature with the Sun or Moon shinning down on you!

The circle defines your ritual area and is intended to create a sacred space for you to work in. It is a space to contain your positive personal power, while shutting out any distracting energies. Hollywood has dramatized this idea to suggest the circle is for keeping out evil spirits or entities that may appear. You are simply creating a sphere of positive energy to work in. What you want to leave outside the circle are all the negative or distracting energies that have pursued you during the day.

The circle is made with personal power that is felt or visualized as streaming from the body. In some traditions a Circle is physically marked on the ground, while in others it is merely visualized. Those who outline their circle may lay stones, flowers or objects on the ground to form their sacred space, or they may simply use a cord or mark a circle on the floor with chalk or salt.

A solitary practitioner may be able to work in a space as small as 3 to 5 feet in diameter, but any comfortable size is fine. In most traditions the circle is oriented to the four quarters with candles or other markers at the north, south, east and west points.

If you choose to use candles, green represents the Earth and is traditionally placed to the North, yellow is placed in the East to represent Air, red or orange symbolizes Fire in the South, and blue is placed in the West to represent Water.

The pentacle, a bowl of salt or earth may also be placed to the North, which is the realm of Earth. The censer and incense or fresh flowers are commonly assigned to the East to acknowledge the realm of Air. To the South, a burning candle represents Fire. Finally, a cup or bowl of water can be placed in the West of the circle, which is the realm of Water.

These objects represent the four elements. If you prefer, they may also be placed on the altar in the center of your circle, in their corresponding directions.

A ceremonial circle is a place in which positive energy and power are kept in, and negative energy is kept out. Some like to use a broom to symbolically sweep the area where the circle will be. Before starting your ritual, you may want to purify yourself as well. Some do this by taking a cleansing bath or shower. Others may simply sprinkle themselves with clean water to symbolize the cleansing.

If you intend to raise energy for a magical purpose, your Circle will allow you to focus on drawing in the energy, and it will contain it until you direct it to its purpose. It also works as a protective barrier to minimize outside distractions.

When you are in the correct frame of mind to do ritual, everything outside your Circle seems to fade away. In the beginning, you don't need to be overly concerned about how strong you cast your circle. If you can see the circle when you look at it, it's strong enough to do the job. In time, you will be able to cast your circle with no visual aids. As you develop your visualization skills, your circle should feel more and more real to you.

This is the basic framework for casting a circle. What you do inside your circle is between you and the Divine. This is your sacred space, a place to connect and commune with the Divine. Speak to the God and Goddess from your heart. Send out energy that is loving, giving and thankful, and watch as your Deities respond in kind!

# Elements and Elementals

"I tell you truly, the Book of Nature is a Holy Scroll ... teach how once again to read from the living pages of the Earthly Mother. For in everything that is life is the law written. It is written in the grass, in the trees, in rivers, mountains, birds of the sky and fishes of the sea." (Excerpt from The Essene Teachings of the Elect)

## The Elements

Earth, Air, Fire and Water are the four elements of nature honored by many paths. Ancient myths and traditions tell us that these four Divine Spirits or Elements were sent to the earth while it was still being formed, to bring about order out of chaos. These four elements are said to link man to nature, and the Divine.

The four elements are still accepted in magic, for they are more closely linked with emotions, the human psyche, and with nature than are modern explanations of the world. These "magical" Earth elements are also of some importance in astrology. Many occultists think of the magical elements as forces, or as "qualities" of energy; especially within the astral world.

Each element has a symbol and color. (Common symbols are -- fire: a triangle pointing up; air: a triangle pointing up and with a horizontal line through the middle of it; water: a triangle pointing down; earth: a triangle pointing down and with a horizontal line through the middle of it.) Colors of the elements are -- earth: brown and green; water: blue; fire: red; air: yellow. The elements are often used in magic ritual.

Magic sees relationships between things. These relationships are called 'correspondences'. Although magical correspondences are not literally equal to one another, you can think of them that way (such as gold equals sun). Thus one thing or symbol can be used to suggest another. This is important in magic, because surrounding yourself with multiple correspondences can enhance the senses.

The magical elements also have correspondences with the four suits of tarot cards, the four quarters (directions of the universe as used in magic ritual) and the Archangels.

## Element Correspondence Table

| Element | Suit | Quarter | Archangel |
| --- | --- | --- | --- |
| Earth | Pentacles | North | Uriel |
| Water | Cups | West | Gabriel |
| Fire | Swords | South | Michael |
| Air | Wands | East | Raphael |

Astrological signs also correspond with the elements. Taurus, Virgo, and Capricorn are earth signs. Cancer, Scorpio, and Pisces are water signs. Aries, Leo and Sagittarius are fire signs. Gemini, Libra, and Aquarius are air signs.

## Elementals

Elementals can be defined as the spirits that inhabit Nature. They are the life-force in all living things, and they exist in the four elements of earth, air, fire, and water, as well as in all the planets and stars above. The belief in their existence was almost universal in the ancient times. Interest in them was especially high in the Middle Ages when practitioners of alchemy and magic sought to acquire nature's secrets and control her forces. Today, this belief still exists among those who believe that all things possess life.

Sometimes fairies and gnomes are included in the elemental category, along with elves and household spirits such as brownies and goblins. Elementals are said to be ruled by higher spirits. In some Witchcraft traditions these higher beings are referred to as Lords of the Watchtowers, the Guardians, or the Mighty Ones. Most Elementals are viewed as benevolent forms that help maintain natural harmony.

Elementals are usually viewed as friendly little spirits of nature. But they are thought by some to be entities of the astral plane, and they are occasionally described as evil or mischievous. These troublesome entities are usually associated with ritual magic and believed to be sent on psychic attacks by magicians. Artificially created elementals are commonly called thought-forms. They are non-physical entities that exist only in the mental or astral plane.

As we mentioned above, worrying about negative or harmful energies will only give them power. Fill your mind with positive, peaceful and loving thoughts, until there is simply no room for negative energies. Harmful thought-forms sent out by others will tend to bounce off and fade away if your own energy is strong. Refer back to PART 4 of this book whenever you need tips on how to raise your energy!

# The Power of the Humble Grass

Below are two excerpts from an ancient writing that I thought you might enjoy. They teach the importance of the humble grass which is one of the precious gifts from the Divine that we tend to take for granted. I hope it gives you a new way to look at, not only the grass beneath your feet, but all the amazing gifts and blessings that your Mother Earth offers you!

*"...And I did moisten a handful of wheat that the angel of Water entered into it. The angel of Air did also embrace it, and the angel of Sun, and the power of the three angels awakened also the angel of Life within the wheat, and sprout and root were born in each grain. Then I put the awakened wheat into the soil of the angel of Earth, and the power of the Earthly Mother and all her angels entered into the wheat, and when the sun had risen four times the grains had become grass. I tell you truly, there is no greater miracle than this."*

The "angels" or messengers of Earth, Air, Fire (Sun) and Water can awaken the your life force as well. These elements have the power to energize your body, clear your mind and renew your spirit. Connect with them daily for a truly magical life!

*"...that most precious gift of your Earthly Mother is the grass beneath your feet, even that grass which you tread upon without thought. Humble and meek is the angel of Earth, for she has no wings to fly, nor golden rays of light to pierce the mist. But great is her strength and vast is her domain, for she covers the earth with her power, and without her the Sons of Men would be no more, for no man can live without the grass, the trees and the plants of the Earthly Mother."*

Today, let your heart be full of joy and gratitude as you walk through the soft grass and commune with your Earthly Mother!

# Wicca & Witchcraft Glossary

In this section you will find a convenient glossary of words commonly used in the practice of Wicca & Witchcraft. Understanding the meaning of these words will prove helpful in your studies as you continue to learn about the Old Ways.

**Adept**: An individual who through serious study and accomplishments is considered highly proficient in a particular magical system.

**Akasha Spirit**: The fifth element, the omnipresent spiritual power that permeates the universe.

**Alchemy**: A branch of High Magic developed in the Middle Ages which sought to magically and/or chemically turn base metals into gold.

**Altar**: A special, flat surface set aside exclusively for magickal workings or religious acknowledgment.

**Amulet**: A magically charged object which deflects specific, usually negative energies. A protective object.

**Ankh**: An Egyptian hieroglyphic widely used as a symbol of life, love, and reincarnation. It is a cross with a looped top.

**Arcana**: The two halves of a tarot deck. The Major Arcana consists of 22 trumps, the Minor Arcana consists of 56 suit cards (sometimes called the lesser or lower Arcana).

**Aspect**: The particular principle or part of the Creative Life Force being worked with or acknowledged at any one time.

**Asperger**: A bundle of fresh herbs or a perforated object used to sprinkle water during or preceding ritual, for purification purposes.

**Astral Plane**: A place which is generally conceptualized as an invisible parallel world which remains unseen from our own solid world of form.

**Astral Travel/Projection**: The process of separating your astral body from your physical one to accomplish travel in the astral plane or dream time.

**Astrology**: The study of and belief in the effects the movements and placements of planets and other heavenly bodies have on the lives and behavior of human beings.

**Athame**: A cleansed and consecrated ritual blade. Usually double edged and black handled. It is never used to cut anything on the physical plane. Pronounced several ways: Ah-THAM-ee ATH-ah-may ah-THAW-may.

**Aura**: The life-energy field which surrounds all living things.

**Automatic Writing**: Form of divination where the channeler uses a pen, paper and an altered state of consciousness to receive messages.

**Balefire**: A fire lit for magickal purposes, usually outdoors. They are traditional on Yule, Beltane, and Midsummer.

**Bane**: That which destroys life, which is poisonous, destructive, dangerous.

**Banish**: To magically end something or exorcise unwanted entities. To rid the presence of.

**Bells**: Often used as ritual tools. They can be used to invoke directional energies, to ring in the sunrise on a Sabbat, or to frighten away faeries and baneful spirits.

**Besom**: A witch's broom.

**Bi-Location**: A type of astral projection during which you maintain awareness of your present surroundings.

**Bind**: To magically restrain something or someone.

**Blue Moon** - Whenever there are two Full Moons in one calendar month, the second is referred to as a Blue Moon.

**Book of Shadows**: A witch's book of spells, rituals, magickal lore. Much akin to a magickal cookbook. Also known as a BOS.

**Boline**: A white-handled knife, used in magick and ritual for purposes such as cutting herbs or piercing a pomegranate.

**Burning Times**: Reference to a historical time from around 1000 C.E. through the 17th century when it is said that up to nine million people were tortured and burned by church and public officials on the assumption that they were the Christian version of Witches. This turned into an extremely profitable venture, as all land and property was seized from the accused individual and portions given to the accuser (in reward fashion) and the remainder seized by the church officials. Historians indicate that the majority of people tortured and murdered were woman and children.

**Call**: Invoking Divine forces.

**Calling the Quarters** - Verbal or symbolic acknowledgment of the Four Elements (Earth, Air, Fire Water) in a ritual environment.

**Cauldron**: Linked to witchcraft in the popular mind, this symbolizes the Goddess, the waters of rebirth.

**Censer**: A heat-proof container in which incense is burned. It is associated with the element air.

**Ceremonial Magick**: A highly codified magickal tradition based upon Kabbala, the Jewish-Gnostic mystical teachings.

**Chakras**: Seven major energy vortexes found in the human body. Each is usually associated with a color. They are: crown - white; third-eye - purple; throat - blue; chest - pink or green; navel - yellow; abdomen - orange; groin - red. Smaller vortexes are located in the hands and feet as well.

**Chalice**: A ritual tool. It represents the female principals of creation.

**Channeling**: A New Age practice wherein you allow a discarnate entity to "borrow" your body to speak to others either through automatic writing or verbally.

**Chaplet:** A crown for the head usually made of flowers and worn at Beltane.

**Charge**: The Originally written in modern form by Doreen Valiente, it is a story of the message from Goddess to Her children.

**Charging**: To infuse an object with personal power.

**Charms**: Either an amulet or talisman that has been charmed by saying an incantation over it and instilling it with energy for a specific task.

**Circle**: Sacred space wherein all magick is to be worked and all ritual contained. It holds ritual energy until the Witch is ready to release it.

**Cleansing**: Removing negative energies from an object or space.

**Collective Unconsciousness**: Term used to describe the sentient connection of all living things, past and present. See also Akashic Records.

**Coming of Age Ritual**: At age 13 for boys, and at the time of a girl's first menses, Pagan children are seen as spiritual adults. The ritual celebrates their new maturity. Generally this is the age when they are permitted membership in covens.

**Cone of Power**: Psychic energy raised and focused by either an individual or group mind (coven) to achieve a definite purpose.

**Conscious Mind**: The analytical, materially-based, rational half of our consciousness. The part of our mind that is at work while we balance our checkbooks, theorize, communicate, and perform other acts related to the physical world.

**Consecration**: The act of blessing an object or place by instilling it with positive energy.

**Correspondence** - An item that has a magickal association. Correspondences include: days, planets, moon phases, herbs, oils, colors, gemstones, Zodiac signs, hours, etc.

**Coven**: A group of thirteen or fewer witches that work together in an organized fashion for positive magickal endeavors or to perform religious ceremonies.

**Covenstead**: The meeting place of witches, often a fixed building or place where the witch can feel safe and at home.

**Craft**: Witchcraft

**Crone**: Aspect of the Goddess represented by the old woman. Symbolized by the waning moon, the carrion crow, the cauldron, the color black. Her Sabbats are Mabon and Samhain.

**Cross-Quarter Days**: Refers to Sabbats not falling on the solstices or equinoxes.

**Days of Power: See Sabbat**. They can also be days triggered by astrological occurrences - your birthday, a woman's menstrual cycle, your dedication/initiation anniversary.

**Dedication**: The process where an individual accepts the Craft as their path and vows to study and learn all that is necessary to reach adept ship. It is a conscious preparation to accept something new into your life and stick with it, regardless of the highs and lows that may follow.

**Deosil**: Clockwise, the direction in which the shadow on a sundial moves as the Sun "moves" across the sky. Deosil is symbolic of life, positive magic and positive energies.

**Dirk**: Ritual knife of the Scottish tradition.

**Divination**: The magickal art of using tools and symbols to gather information from the Collective Unconsciousness. This can be on people, places, things and events past, present, and future.

**Divine Power**: The pure energy that exists within the Goddess and God. The life force, the ultimate source of all things.

**Dowsing**: The divinatory art of using a pendulum or stick to find the actual location of a person, place, thing, or element.

**Drawing Down the Moon**: A ritual performed during the Full Moon by witches to empower themselves and unite their essence with a particular deity, usually the Goddess.

**Drawing Down the Sun**: Lesser-known and lesser-used companion ritual to Drawing Down the Moon in which the essence of the Sun God is drawn into the body of a male witch.

**Duality**: The opposite of polarity. When used as a religious term, it separates two opposites such as good and evil and places those characteristics into two completely separate God-forms.

**Earth Magick**: The energy that exists within stones, herbs, flames, wind, and other natural objects.

**Earth Plane**: Metaphor for your normal waking consciousness, or for the everyday, solid world we live in.

**Elements**: Usually: Earth, air, fire, water. The building blocks of the universe. Everything that exists contains one or more of these energies. Some include a fifth element- spirit or Akasha.

**Elementals**: Archetypical spirit beings associated with one of the four elements. Elementals are sometimes called Faeries.

**Enchantment**: A magickal object that must be kept absolutely secret and hidden from all human eyes and affects a hidden aura. They must be charmed first. Gems and magickal writing are good items to use.

**Eostre's Eggs**: Colored, decorated eggs of Ostara; named for the Teutonic Goddess Eostre. AKA Easter eggs.

**Esbat**: A gathering or ritual usually occurring on the Full Moon and dedicated to the Goddess in her lunar aspect.

**Evocation**: To call something out from within.

**Faerie**: See Elemental

**Faerie Burgh**: Mound of earth which covers a faerie colony's underground home.

**Familiar**: An animal that has a spiritual bone with a witch; many times a family witch. Familiars can also be entities that dwell on the astral plane.

**Fascination**: A mental effort to control another animal or person's mind. Also known as "mind-bending". Often considered unethical.

**Folklore**: Traditional sayings, cures, faerie tales, and folk wisdom of a particular locale which is separate from their mythology.

**Folk Magick**: The Practice of projecting personal power, as well as the energies within natural objects such as herbs, and crystals, to bring about needed changes.

**Gaea/Gaia**: Mother Earth.

**God**: Masculine aspect of deity.

**Goddess**: Feminine aspect of deity.

**Grain Dolly**: Figure usually woven at Imbolc from dried sheaves of grain collected at the previous harvest. The dolly is traditionally burned at Yule and a new one made the following Imbolc.

**Great Rite**: Symbolic sexual union (also sacred marriage) of the Goddess and God that is enacted at Beltane in many traditions, and other Sabbats in other traditions. It symbolizes the primal act of creation from which all life comes.

**Green Man**: Another name for the God

**Grimoire**: A magickal workbook containing ritual information, formulae, magickal properties of natural objects and preparation of ritual equipment. Often used interchangeably with Book of Shadows.

**Grounding**: To disperse excess energy generated during magickal work by sending it into the earth. It also means the process of centering one's self in the physical world both before and after any ritual or astral experience.

**Grove**: Synonymous with coven.

**Guardians**: Ceremonial magicians use the Guardians of the Watchtowers or Four Quarters. Some witches use them, too.

**Hand Fasting**: A Pagan wedding.

**Herbalism**: Art of using herbs to facilitate human needs both magically and medicinally.

**Higher Self**: That part of us which connects our corporeal minds to the Collective Unconscious and with the divine knowledge of the universe.

**Hiving Off**: This term is used for a small coven which splits off from a larger one. Sometimes this is done to keep the gatherings of a manageable size, other times covens split over philosophical differences.

**Horned God**: One of the most prevalent God-images in Paganism. NOT Satan or the Devil!!!

**Initiation**: A process whereby an individual is introduced or admitted into a coven. Usually a ritual occasion. Not to be confused with dedication.

**Incense**: Ritual burning of herbs, oils, or other aromatic items to scent the air during acts of magic and ritual, and to better help the witch attune to the goal of the working. **Invocation**: To bring something in from without.

**Karma**: The belief that one's thoughts and deeds can either be counted against them or added to their spiritual path across several life times.

**Kabbala**: Mystical teaching from the Jewish-Gnostic tradition. Ceremonial Magic and the Alexandrian traditions are based in these teachings. Also, Qabalah.

**Labrys**: A double-headed ax which symbolizes the Goddess in Her Lunar aspect. Has roots in ancient Crete.

**Left-Hand Path**: Refers to the practice of using magick to control others, to change the will of others, for personal gain. Generally frowned upon by true Wiccans and Witch's. Dark Magic.

**Libation**: Ritually given portion of food or drink to a deity, nature spirit, or ghost.

**Macrocosm**: The world around us.

**Magick/Magic**: The projection of natural energies (such as personal power) to bring about needed change. Magic is the process of raising this energy, giving it purpose, and releasing it. Some choose to spell magic with a "K" on the end. This spelling was made popular by Aleister Crowley in the 1900's to differentiate it from the stage magic performed in that time. Some believe that Magic is evil and should not be tampered with, or that it is only possessed by "chosen" ones. Both of these statements are false.

**Magic Circle**: A sphere constructed of personal power in which rituals are usually performed. Within it the witch is protected from outside forces. The sphere extends both above and below the surface of the ground.

**Magical System**: The basic set of guidelines relating to the worship of specific Gods and Goddesses or cultural traditions.

Male Mysteries: Pagan study which attempts to reclaim the power and mystery of the old Gods for today's Pagan males.

**Matrifocal**: Term used to denote pre-patriarchal life when family clans centered around and lived near or on clan matriarch.

**May Pole**: Sexual symbol of Beltane representing the phallus.

**Meditation**: Reflection, contemplation- turning inward toward the self, or outward toward Deity or nature. A quiet time in which the practitioner may either dwell upon particular thoughts or symbols, or allow them to come unbidden.

**Megalith**: A huge stone monument or structure. Stonehenge is the best-known example of a megalith.

**Menhir**: A huge stone probably erected by early peoples for religious, spiritual, or magickal reasons.

**Microcosm**: The world within us.

**Monotheism**: Belief in one supreme deity who has no other forms and/of displays no other aspects.

**Mother**: The aspect of the Goddess representing motherhood, mid-life, and fertility. She is represented by the full moon, the egg, and the colors red and green. Her Sabbats are Midsummer and Lughnasadh.

**Myth**: Cycles Body of lore about any land or people that makes up their mythology.

**New Age**: The mixing of metaphysical practices with a structured religion.

**Nursery Rhyme**: Cute doggerel or poems supposedly written for the amusement of children. Much Pagan lore was hidden in these ditties during the years of witch persecutions.

**Occult**: Literal meaning is "hidden" and is broadly applied to a wide range of metaphysical topics which lie outside the accepted realm of mainstream theologies.

**Occultist**: One who practices and or studies a variety of occult subjects.

**Ogham**: Celtic equivalent of the Teutonic runes. The ancient alphabet of the Celtic people.

**Old Ones**: The A term which refers to all aspects of the Goddess and God.

**Old Religion**: A name for Paganism as it pre-dates Christianity by at least 20,000 years. Also referred to as the Old Ways.

**Pagan/Neo-Pagan**: General term for followers of Wicca and other magickal, shamanistic, and polytheistic Earth-based religions. Also used to refer to pre-Christian religious and magickal systems.

**Paganing**: When a baby is presented in circle to the Goddess and God, and given a craft name which s/he will keep until about 13 and can choose their own at their Coming of Age celebration.

**Pantheon**: A collection or group of Gods and Goddesses in a particular religious or mythical structure.

**Pantheism**: Belief in many deities who are really one because they are all merely aspects of the single creative life source. Paganism is pantheistic.

**Passion Over Ritual**: Ritual observed when a loved one dies.

**Past-Life Regression**: Act of using meditation or guided meditation to pass through the veil of linear time and perceive experiences encountered in a previous existence.

**Path Working**: Using astral projection, bi-location, or dream time to accomplish a specific goal. Also called vision questing.

**Patriarchal**: Term used to apply to the world since the matrifocal clans that worshipped Goddesses were supplanted by codified religions that honor all-male deity(s).

**Pendulum**: A divinatory device consisting of a string attached to a heavy object, such as a quartz crystal, root, or ring. The free end of the string is held in the hand, the elbows steadied against a flat surface, and a question is asked. The movement of the heavy object's swings determines the answer. It is a tool which contacts the psychic mind.

**Pentacle**: A circle surrounding a five-pointed, upright star (pentagram). Worn as a symbol of a witch's beliefs. Many witches consider wearing it inverted to be blasphemy of their faith and is commonly associated with Satanism.

**Pentagram**: The basic interlaced five-pointed star, visualized with one point up. It represents the five elements: Earth, Air, Fire, Water, and Spirit. It is a symbol of power and protection.

**Personal Power**: The energy which sustains our bodies. It originates within the Goddess and God. We first absorb it from our biological mother within the womb, and later from food, water, the Moon and Sun, and other natural objects.

**Polarity**: The concept of equal, opposite energies. The Eastern Yin Yang is a perfect example. Yin is cold; yang is hot. Other examples: Goddess/God, night/day, Moon/Sun, birth/death, dark/light, psychic mind/unconscious mind. Universal balance.

**Polytheism**: Belief in the existence of many unrelated deities each with their own dominion and interests who have no spiritual or familial relationships to one another.

**Poppets**: Anthropomorphic dolls used to represent certain human beings in magick spells.

**Projective Hand**: The hand thought to be the point through which personal power is sent from the body. Normally the hand used for manual activities such as writing, dialing the phone, etc. It is also the hand in which tools such as the athame and wand are held.

**Psychic Mind**: The subconscious or unconscious mind, in which we receive psychic impressions. It is at work when we sleep, dream, and meditate. It is our direct link with the Divine, and with the larger, nonphysical world around us.

**Psychism**: The act of being consciously psychic, in which the psychic mind and conscious mind are linked and working in harmony. Also known as psychic awareness.

**Qabalah**: See Kabbala

**Receptive Hand**: The hand through which energy is received into the body. The left hand in right-handed persons, the reverse for left-handed persons.

**Rede**: The Basic tenet of witchcraft. "An it harm none, do what thou will.

**Reincarnation**: The process of repeated incarnations in human form to allow evolution of the sexless, ageless soul.

**Ritual Ceremony**: A specific form of movement, a manipulation of objects or inner processes designed to produce desired effects. In religion ritual is geared toward union with the Divine. In magickal works it produces a specific state of consciousness that allows the magician to move energy toward needed goals.

**Ritual Consciousness**: A specific, alternate state of awareness necessary to the successful practice of magick. This state is achieved through the use of visualization and ritual. The conscious mind becomes attuned with the psychic mind, a state in which the magician senses energies, gives them purpose, and releases them toward a specific goal. It is a heightening of senses, an expanded awareness of the nonphysical world, a linking with nature and with Deity.

**Ritual Tools**: General name for magickal tools used by a witch or magician. They vary by tradition and usually represent one of the elements.

**Runes**: A set of symbols used both in divination and magickal work. There are several types will different origins- Scandinavian, Norse, Germanic.

**Sabbat**: A witch's festival.

**Scourge**: Small device made from leather or hemp which resembles a whip and is used in flagellation rites within some traditions.

**Scrying**: A method of divination. To gaze at or into an object (a quartz crystal sphere, a pool of water, reflections, a candle flame) to still the conscious mind in order to contact the psychic mind. Scrying allows the scryer to become aware of events prior to their actual occurrence, as well as to perceive past or present events through other than the five senses.

**Shaman**: A man or woman who has obtained knowledge of the subtler dimensions of the Earth, usually through periods of alternate states of consciousness. Various types of ritual allow the shaman to pierce the veil of the physical world and to experience the realm of energies. This knowledge lends the shaman the power to change his or her world through magick.

**Shamanism**: The practice of shamans, usually ritualistic or magickal in nature, sometimes religious.

**Shillelagh**: Magickal tool corresponding to the staff in other traditions. Usually made from blackthorn wood.

**Sigil**: Magically oriented seal, sign, glyph, or other device used in a magickal working. Ones you create yourself are the most effective. Sigils can be used on letters, packages, clothing, etc.

**Simple Feast**: A ritual meal shared with the Goddess and God.

**Sky Father**: Shamanistic in origin. It refers to the sky, or that which is above us, as a masculine deity.

**Skyclad**: The act of celebrating or performing magickal works in the nude. Considered deeply spiritual, NOT sexual.

**Solitary**: Pagan who works and worships alone.

**Spell**: A magical ritual or concentrated form of energy, usually non-religious in nature and often accompanied by spoken words. It should always be clear, concise, focused and emotional.

**Spiral**: Symbol of coming into being.

**Staff**: Ritual tool which corresponds to the wand or athame.

**Subconscious Mind**: Part of the mind which functions below the levers we are able to access in the course of a normal working day. This area stores symbolic knowledge, dreams, the most minute details of every experience ever had by a person.

**Summerland**: The Pagan Land of the Dead.

**Sympathetic Magic**: Concept of likes attract. Most common way spells are worked.

**Talisman**: An object charged with personal power to attract a specific force or energy to its bearer.

**Tarot Cards**: Set of 78 cards which feature pictures and symbols used to conned the diviner with the collective unconscious.

**Threefold Law**: Karmic principle that energy that is released is returned three times over.

**Tradition**: Branch of paganism followed by any individual Pagan or coven.

**Trilithon**: A stone arch made from two upright slabs with one lying atop these. They are featured in Stonehenge.

**Triple Goddess**: One Goddess in all of her three aspects: Maiden, Mother, Crone.

**Virgin**: Youngest aspect of the Triple Goddess. Also known as the Maiden. Represented by the waxing moon, colors white and blue. Her Sabbats are Imbolc and Ostara.

**Vision Quest**: Using astral projection, bi-location, or dream time to accomplish a specific goal. Also called path working.

**Visualization**: The process of forming mental images. Magickal visualization consists of forming images of needed goals during ritual. It is also used to direct personal power and natural energies for various purposes during magick, including charging and forming of the magick circle.

**Wand**: Ritual tool brought to the craft from ritual magick.

**Warlock**: Antiquated term misused in reference to a male Witch. It means oath-breaker or Liar. Most Pagans, Witch's find the term offensive.

**Web Weaving**: Networking with other magickal people via conversation, writing, e-mail, to gather information which will mutually assist each party.

**Wheel of the Year**: One full cycle of the seasonal year.

**Wicca**: A modern Pagan religion with spiritual roots in the earliest expressions of reverence for nature. Some major identifying motifs are: reverence for both the Goddess and God; acceptance of reincarnation and magic; ritual observance of astronomical and agricultural phenomena; and the use of magical circles for ritual purposes.

**Wicce**: Synonymous with Wicca. In some circles, Wicce is used for women and Wicca is used for men.

**Widdershins**: Counter-clockwise motion, usually used for negative magical purposes, or for dispersing negative energies or conditions such as disease.

**Witch**: A practitioner of folk magick, particularly that kind relating to herbs, stones, colors, wells, rivers, etc. It is used by some Wiccans to describe themselves. This term has nothing to do with Satanism.

**Witchcraft**: The craft of the witch- magick, especially magick utilizing personal power in conjunction with the energies within stones, herbs, colors, and other natural objects. This belief system also has nothing to do with Satanism.

**Yggdrasil**: One of the best known Tree of Life symbols. It unites all existence from the Underworld, to the Physical world.

## ADDITIONAL RESOURCES

If you're on Facebook, visit our Living Wicca Today page at: https://www.facebook.com/living.wicca.today  This is a great place to connect with others who practice the Old Ways!

To receive a **FREE** subscription to the Inner Circle Newsletter visit: http://wicca.com/publications/free.html *This complimentary publication explores the ancient spiritual wisdom of Wicca, Witchcraft and Pagan traditions and it keeps you updated on any helpful new articles or books we publish about the Old Ways. **Welcome to the Inner Circle**!*

**The Celtic Connection** offers a magical home to all who are seeking a spiritual connection with Nature and our Mother Earth.  You can explore links to several hundred pages about Wicca and Witchcraft traditions, Paganism, Shamanism and Druid lore. You'll also find information on Pagan holidays, moon phases, candle magic, healing herbs, animal guides, meditation and more.  Then get the Pagan books, Wiccan jewelry, gifts and magical supplies you need in our Wicca stores. Please explore freely.  Thank you for your interest in Wicca and the Old Ways.  **http://wicca.com**

*May the God and Goddess bless you on your journey!*

## *ABOUT THE AUTHOR*

Kardia Zoe is a native Oregonian and co-founder of one of the oldest and largest information sites for Wicca and Witchcraft on the Internet. The website averages over 2,000 unique visitors per day and she has been providing these guests with guidance since 1997.

Now, in her Living Wicca Today series, Kardia is sharing her years of insight into this beautiful Earth religion as she addresses the most frequently asked questions about Wicca and gives you a clear, accurate understanding of the traditional beliefs and practices. Her books dispel the lingering myths and misconceptions that surround this religion, so you can move forward with confidence on an amazing journey into the enchanted word of Wicca.

# e-Books by Kardia Zoe you may enjoy!

 *Book #1 Wiccan & Pagan Holidays*
http://www.amazon.com/dp/B00PZCMT3O

 *Book # 2 Wicca: A Beginner's Guide to Earth Magic*
http://www.amazon.com/dp/B00QSPXTMW

 Book #3 Wicca: A Beginner's Guide to Casting Spells
**Release Date: 12/21/2014**

Book #4 Taking to the Goddess: The Power of Intuition & Divination - *Release Date: February 1, 2015*

**Enriching Your Life With Wicca**: An Essential Guide to the Wiccan Path for Beginners and Solitary Practitioners.

*Release Date: March 20, 2015*

CPSIA information can be obtained at www.ICGtesting.com
Printed in the USA
LVOW04s1100110115

422376LV00001B/303/P